Forecasting Pharmaceutical Sales: An Evidence Based Approach

by Gary Johnson

London Scientific Publishing, Henley on Thames

Published by London Scientific Publishing
an imprint of Inpharmation Ltd.
Long Meadow, Spurgrove Lane, Frieth, Henley on Thames, England, RG9 6NU
Email info@inpharmation.co.uk
Web www.inpharmation.co.uk

A CIP catalogue record for this book is available from the British Library.

ISBN:0-9534404-2-7

Printed in Malta

For Harry, the most welcome of unforecast events.

About the Author

Gary Johnson is Managing Director of Inpharmation. He has worked in the pharmaceutical industry for two decades in sales management, marketing management, general management and heading global marketing.

He is a best selling management author. He has been a finalist in the prestigious MCA Book Prize and a semi-finalist in the FT World Book Prize.

He has appeared frequently in broadcast and printed media and is a sought after speaker at industry conferences.

He holds degrees in medical science from Nottingham University Medical School and management from London Business School where he is also a Sloan Fellow.

Gary Johnson has been researching and experimenting with pharmaceutical forecasting methods for decades. This book pulls together the key lessons that this quest has uncovered.

The aim of this book

Around 100 years ago, medicine was highly ineffective ('I can treat syphilis and very little else') and marketing highly inefficient ('I know half my marketing is wasted - but which half?')

Today medicine is being transformed - largely by the successes of the pharmaceutical industry. But marketing remains amazingly inefficient and *increasingly* ineffective.

This is largely due to the lack of excellent training for practitioners. It takes around 10,000 hours to become expert in something. Doctors train for that long. But, today, many pharmaceutical product managers are practising after less than 100 hours training.

As a result, they are at the mercy of consultants, market research agencies and advertising agencies who profess marketing 'expertise' but are actually experts at maximising *their* revenues.

This book, along with the others in the 'Evidence Based' series, aims to address this gap and to put companies back in charge of their marketing strategies.

List of contents

Introduction: The problem with forecasting

Forecasting in the pharmaceutical industry could be done *much* better. This book gives you the principles and techniques you need to make your forecasts the best they can reasonably be. But you need more than just the best techniques. There are all sorts of barriers to effective forecasting out there. These range from a lack of understanding of what forecasting is and what it can do to a reluctance to accept unpalatable truths. So, before we get lost in the fascinating detail of how to produce the best forecasts, we face up to these problems and look at some ways you can deal with them.

The costs of inaccurate forecasting in the pharmaceutical industry

Is there a need for better sales forecasting in the pharmaceutical industry? The answer lies in the costs of the inaccuracy of current forecasts. These include: When sales forecasts are too high: stock write-offs, unnecessary capital investment in factories and plant, wasted R&D and licensing and marketing costs for non-viable products. When sales forecasts are too low: stock outs, increased manufacturing costs (overtime, increased material and contractors fees through rushed jobs etc.) and lost revenues from viable products wrongly terminated, not licensed or not launched.

Let's try and put a number on it.

R&D costs around 15% of sales. Only one in five R&D projects generates more value than the costs of development[1]. On average, the other four return around half their costs. If just half of this cost is due to poor forecasting (pursuing demonstrably non-viable products), that equates to 6% of sales.

Manufacturing represents around 20% of sales. It is estimated that around 20% of costs could be saved with perfect sales forecasts[2]. i.e. another 4% of sales.

Marketing represents around 30% of sales. Faulty forecasts result in the wrong products being promoted or products having inappropriate promotional spends. Lord Leverhulme famously said that 'half my advertising is wasted, I just don't know which half' (although in the US the same remark is attributed to John Wanamaker). I believe the situation is *at least* this bad in pharmaceuticals. But, let's be charitable and say that only a third is wasted. That represents another 10% of sales.

So, the direct costs of inaccurate sales forecasts *could* be in the order of 20% of sales. (Which is around the profit margin of the industry, suggesting that the savings from accurate forecasts could double our profits.)

Then there is the indirect cost - opportunity cost - of foregone development projects, foregone promotional campaigns etc., etc.. Whatever the real value, the cost of inaccurate forecasts to this industry is massive. And how much does the pharmaceutical industry spend on forecasting?

A US survey - published in the Harvard Business Review some time ago[3] - suggested that, in the US, firms with a turnover of $10 million spent about 2% of it on forecasting, while $1 billion firms spent 0.1%. Pharmaceutical companies tend towards the lower end of this range[4]. An increased investment in forecasting could certainly be justified. However, the good news is that the problem is not the spend, but *the quality* of the forecasting. Indeed, often better forecasts could be produced for less money than is currently spent.

In order for you to make better forecasts, it will help to understand the problems that cause poor forecasting. Some of the most important problems and misunderstandings are covered below.

Forecasting is a new discipline and can therefore appear a confused discipline

Forecasting is a relatively modern speciality. Almost all the significant work in the field has been done since 1960[5]. Because forecasting is so new, the area is full of confusion. People have spent far more time coming up with all sorts of models and methodologies than they have establishing which ones really work and in what circumstances. Therefore, you can spend a lot of time learning about techniques that do not work. (This work is an attempt to start to put that right as far as pharmaceuticals is concerned).

Indeed, you can spend a lot of time trying to forecast things that cannot be forecast...

Forecasting versus futurology

Because the evidence base for forecasting is so poorly understood, forecasting elicits mixed emotions. Some people think all forecasters are charlatans. Some people see forecasting as the ultimate in strategic vision. Some people can't make up their mind what they think:

> The great Peter Druker once said that 'Forecasting is not a respectable human activity',
> but then went on to write America's Next Twenty Years.

So, I would like to start by being very clear about what we mean here by 'forecasting'. In particular, I would like to draw a very clear distinction between 'forecasting' and 'futurology'. By forecasting, I mean predicting the sales of existing or development stage pharmaceuticals whose profiles are known (ideally precisely, but at least within a modest range of possibilities) in a market place that is not radically dissimilar to the current one.

By futurology, I mean predicting revolutionary changes in healthcare technology (including which pharmaceutical research streams will bear fruit) and the healthcare environment. Futurologists encourage you to gaze forwards into a murky future that only they can see. But, if you spend a little time looking back at the records for their past predictions, you can save yourself the bother. Just consider the pitiful record of 'futurologists' over the decades.

Experts have wrongly forecast the success of the following innovations over the past forty years: video telephones, dehydrated foods, ultrasonic dishwashers and showers, voice recognition, jet-engined cars, habitable lunar bases, personal vertical take-off planes, 3-D television, commercial passenger rockets, usable nuclear fusion. And so on *ad nauseam.*

Not only have the technological forecasters committed sins of commission, they have committed just as many sins of omission. Innovations that were not predicted include, the light bulb, the radio, aeroplanes, television, radar, atomic energy, jet propulsion, space travel, cellular phones, compact discs and GUI (the point-and-click graphical user interface that we all use on our computers). Indeed experts even failed to predict the widespread use of the computer itself. As late as 1950, the dictionary definition of computer was 'someone who computes'.

The truth of this principle is perhaps even more apparent within the field of healthcare and pharmaceuticals. In the early 1970s forty men - each expert within their field - gathered under the auspices of the Office of Health Economics. Their mission was to predict the state of health and health care in the 1990s[6]. Some of their expert prognostications included:

- The widespread legitimate use of recreational drugs like marijuana and LSD
- The ability to fully control 70% of cancers
- The ability to predict heart attacks days in advance
- Drugs which dissolve away dangerous clots
- The perfection of artificial hearts
- The control of world-wide pharmaceutical research, production and marketing in the hands of a dozen or two companies (an old favourite with futurologists)

(Well, at least they got the clot-busters right!)

> The unpredictability of medical advances is a general phenomenon. William Ascher[7] reviewed collections of expert forecasts across a number of fields. He found that the greatest spread - and therefore the minimum possible typical error even if the forecasts were right on average - was for medical therapy.

Unfortunately, most of the money spent on forecasting is spent on this hopeless futurology. It has been estimated that each year the 'prediction industry' sells around $200 billion worth of (mostly inaccurate) forecasts[8]. These are the books by Alvin Toffler that tell of future shock, but whose most shocking aspect is the dismal inaccuracy of the forecasts[8]. These are the computer programs sold by merchant banks to help investors predict currency crashes, but the only money made is by the sellers of these ineffective programs[9]. These are the pharmaceutical industry reports that tell of the demise of the pharmaceutical industry because of managed care, but the only demise has been for the scare stories[10]. These are the forecasts that give forecasting a bad name.

So, our aims here are modest. We are not crystal ball gazing. We are trying to predict how known products will sell in a known healthcare environment. That is hard enough!

Forecasting is not *always* the correct solution to your problem

If the forecast required for your particular business problem involves 'futurology', then – given that futurology is so inaccurate – you ought to consider the alternatives. For there *are* perfectly respectable and proper alternatives to forecasting:

- You may be able to hedge against possible futures by taking out insurance or by having contingency plans. For example, it is virtually impossible to predict which drugs will succeed and which will fail during the development process (other than knowing the rough risks as the various stages). But, a large diversified development portfolio can go some way to spreading the risk.
- You may be able to control the future in which case you do not need to forecast (just as you do not need to be able to forecast the weather inside your own house). For example, if you are structuring an in-license deal and much of the money you pay is in the form of up-front payments, you need accurate sales forecasts. Whereas, if you structure an in-licensing agreement so that most of the money is in the form of royalties, (which only arise on sales made) you are much more in control. Accurate forecasts become less vital. It is easier for you to 'suck the product and see'.
- If you can respond easily and quickly, you do not need to be able to forecast (just as you do not need forecasts of every bend in the road ahead when driving your car). For example, you are launching a new product internationally. Your production director has produced launch stocks and is stocking them as bulk. He can pack them into the pack for any given country in just two weeks. You now don't have to forecast the exact country by country split with any great accuracy. (Which is just as well because generally the inaccuracy of forecasts increases as you try to forecast for smaller and smaller segments.)

In deciding whether you need to spend a lot of effort forecasting, there are a couple of things that you should bear in mind. First try an *a fortiori* analysis. Say you are deciding whether to continue a project or not and that you are in doubt over the exact market size. Before you pay to find out the exact market size, try assuming that the market is as big as it could reasonably be. If the analysis says you should *not* do it, then given that the real market size is almost certainly smaller than the one that you have assumed, you should very certainly not do it. Your conclusion is even stronger ('*a fortiori*') than the one you would reach if you spent a lot of effort forecasting.

Second, consider the cost-benefit ratio of the decision your forecast is supporting. If the costs of pursuing an opportunity are low, or the potential upside very high, then it might still be worth pursuing the project even if an honest forecast of the most likely potential suggests you should stop. The less confidence you have in a forecast and the greater the possible upside if the forecast is wrong, the more you should be inclined to ignore the forecast and prefer suck-it-and-see.

Another way to think about the costs and benefits of listening to or ignoring forecasts is shown in the following table:

ONE WAY OF LOOKING AT WHETHER TO USE FORECASTS

	Company decides "go"	Company decides "stop"
Forecast says "go"		Cost of lost opportunity Benefit of saved investment
Forecast says "stop"	Cost of lost investment Benefit of unexpected success	

You can easily lose sight of what you are trying to achieve

The next difficulty is that there has been so much attention on complicated methodologies in forecasting that it is sometimes not clear to users what the methodology is actually designed to *do*. It is particularly unfortunate that methods tend to be named after the statistical techniques employed rather than the task that they are designed to accomplish. For example 'conjoint analysis'. Conjoint analysis is one of a number of techniques for uncovering the 'rules' that people use when making decisions. In pharmaceutical forecasting, this generally means discovering which product attributes drive the choices that doctors *say* they would make in a paper and pencil exercise. Put this way, the issues surrounding the use of conjoint analysis in forecasting become apparent:

- What bearing does such information have on what doctors will actually do in the real world?
- What other factors are also important?

So, throughout your forecasting, don't let the means become an end in itself. Keep asking yourself:

1. What you are trying to do?
2. What – in plain language – does the technique you are considering actually do? and
3. How does 2. Relate to 1?

There are no magic bullets in forecasting

But even with the right approach, there is no 'perfect way' to make a forecast. Having been immersed in forecasting for many years, US academic Stephen Schnaars concludes, 'People want to believe in magic bullets in forecasting. They do not exist.'[11]

Jerry Jackson, head of international marketing at Merck in 1991, gave two examples of how easily forecasts can go wrong. Merck's hepatitis B vaccine was aimed at health workers and at the gay community. But the AIDS scare meant health workers were afraid to use a product derived from human plasma and the gay community were diffuse and hard to target. Sales were a quarter of the forecast. On the other hand, Clinoral was launched on a slow news day and a modest press release was picked up by the doyen of

American news broadcasters, Walter Cronkite. This time early sales were four times higher than forecast. Jackson admits that: 'Despite all the sophisticated technology, if we are plus or minus twenty-five percent in the first year we consider ourselves lucky.'[12]

This book will not deliver magic bullets but, will make getting into the +/- 25% range much less of a matter of luck. The keys to improving your forecasting hit rate lie – as you will see – in:

- A few proven principles
- A handful of validated models
- A great deal of thought into the assumptions you make and
- An open-minded and humble attitude

Your forecasts will not always be popular

Your difficulties don't end when you have produced what you believe to be a good forecast. A good forecast is often unpopular. It has been said that the only useful advice is unwelcome advice. (Welcome advice tends to confirm existing prejudices.) The problem is that unwelcome advice tends to be rejected or ignored.

Paradoxically, evidence that contradicts people's strongly held beliefs tends to strengthen that belief. A classic study[13] demonstrated this counterintuitive truth back in 1975.

Members of a church youth group were told that their views were needed as part of a vital piece of market research. Archaeologists had unearthed documents that had turned out to be correspondence between the apostles. However, the New York Times - under pressure from the World Council of Churches - was withholding the story in a Watergate-type cover up. Now, the New York Times was conducting this market research to gauge what the impact of releasing the contents of these documents would be.

The documents showed that the apostles had realised that, since Christ had died, the public would realise that he was not God. But, they believed that people wanted to believe Christ was God and so they had created a deception of the resurrection to fool them.

The youth group members now completed a second questionnaire to indicate how strongly they believed in God. Amazingly, this disconfirming evidence led believers to *increase* the strength of their conviction that Christ is God. Furthermore, the increase was greatest in those who had held the strongest belief in the first place. And, even more surprisingly, the increase was strongest for the people who believed the documents were authentic.

How to "sell" your forecasts

So, you are going to have to sell your forecasts if you want people to take them on board and change their outlooks. The answer is not fancy presentations and cutesy graphics.

There is evidence that complex presentation and visual aids do not help understanding and recall. For example, it has been shown that TV weather forecasts with all those amazing visual aids do not result in any better recall of forecasts, even in motivated individuals. At least a part of the problem is that there is too much irrelevant or extraneous information. Indeed, as the length of these forecasts increases, the amount of information retained stays about the same[14]. (Although, of course, the proportion of the information retained declines.)

Also, surprisingly, there is considerable evidence that graphics are no more effective in engendering understanding and recall than tables[15].

So, what is the answer? The key message from all the work that has been done in change management is: *People who are affected by change should be put in control of the change where possible.* So, don't try to sell the results of your forecasts after you have done all the work. Get people to buy into your process and your methodologies at the outset. Better still get them *involved* in producing the forecasts.

The realisation that involvement leads to action is not a recent one. Nor is it unique to pharmaceuticals.

In a classic 1947 study Lewin[16] compared lecture versus group decision in trying to get housewives to use various new foods. Group decision worked better. Two other classic studies from the 50s showed the same impact from involvement for factory workers[17] and college students[18].

One way to get people involved in all the possible outcomes of your forecasting is to get them to consider different scenarios, before the results of the forecast are known. There is evidence that this works.

Larry Gregory and co-workers[19] conducted four fascinating experiments on scenarios. Each experiment involved asking people how likely something was to happen: being arrested for armed robbery (irrespective of whether you are guilty or not); winning a vacation trip; being arrested for shoplifting and subscribing to cable TV in the next six weeks. But some of the people were asked straight out, while others were asked to imagine scenarios whereby the event could occur before answering the question. The people who had imagined the scenarios rated these events - on average - as more than twice as likely to happen than the people who had not imagined scenarios.

These, then, are some of the problems that you face in forecasting. We now move onto the solutions. Before we get lost in the details of specific techniques, it is important that you understand the principles that underlie all effective forecasts. These principles are the subject of the first chapter.

Chapter 1: The six principles of good forecasting

Expedients are for the hour,
But principles are for the ages.
Henry Ward Beecher

Although there are specific models and methods that have proven to be effective in forecasting pharmaceutical sales, there are a set of principles that are as – perhaps more - important.   And, it is necessary to understand these principles in order to select, apply and interpret the various models and methods effectively.

We therefore start with a review of the principles of good forecasting. These principles are based on evidence. Some of that evidence is presented here. But, when we cover the specific techniques and models, *much more evidence of these principles will emerge.*

Principle 1: Break the Problem Down

On July 16th 1945, a plutonium bomb – the world's first nuclear weapon – was exploded in the New Mexico desert. Before readings from the many scientific instruments were analysed, one of the scientists involved, Enrico Fermi, knew that its power, equivalent to around 20,000 tons of TNT, had vastly exceeded all expectations. Fermi had reputedly estimated the power of the bomb by casting a handful of torn up paper into the blast from the bomb and observing how far the pieces had been blown. He then calculated the bomb's power by breaking the problem down into many parts. Roughly how massive were the bits of paper? Roughly how far had they been blown? Roughly what speed of wind would be needed to do this? Roughly how far was he from the bomb? Roughly how quickly did the blast drop off as it moved out from the bomb? …. And so on. Fermi is said to have attributed the remarkable accuracy of his estimate to the fact that *when a problem is broken down into many parts, the inaccuracies in the many assumptions tend to cancel each other out.* (An estimate that is made by breaking a problem down and combining a range of 'sub-estimates' is still known as a Fermi Calculation.)

Breaking a problem down into its constituent parts is known in the forecasting literature as 'decomposition'. Decomposition offers another major benefit on top of Fermi's point in that it spreads risk (errors in one part of the forecast tend to offset errors in another). It allows different expertise and methods to be brought to the separate parts of the problem.

Evidence suggests that decomposition is particularly useful in helping judgmental decisions and in circumstances where uncertainty is high.

For example, researchers in a 1975 study[20] asked people a number of questions, such as 'How many packs of Polaroid colour film were used in the United States in 1970?' But the question was asked in two ways. Either in its whole form or in a decomposed form. So, for example, the Polaroid question above would be broken down into: What is the population of the USA? How many people per family? What proportion of families own cameras? What proportion of these own Polaroids? How many packs of film a year do they use? What proportion of these are colour film?

Inevitably, the decomposed version of the question yielded more accurate answers.

§

The same improvement has been found as far as purchasing intentions are concerned. In 1980, Paul Warshaw[21] asked sixty consumers about their intentions to buy various soft drinks over a five day period. He asked in a global way: 'How likely are you to buy brand X between now and next Monday morning?'. And he asked in a decomposed way: 'How likely are you to go to the supermarket?...How likely are you to buy these various brands?...'

The decomposed question (which Warshaw calls the 'derived intention') was significantly better at predicting actual purchases than the global question.

The fact that decomposition results in better forecasts explains why forecasting by assuming a value share of a particular market is such an inaccurate approach. Sales value can easily be decomposed. To take the most banal example: sales value can be decomposed into sales volume and price. Take the hypertension market:

Assume that it is 1990 and you are trying to forecast how big the market for ACE inhibitors will be in the USA. If you look at the anti-hypertensives market in value terms, you would have seen the following picture:

US ANTI-HYPERTENSIVES MARKET 1990: VALUE ONLY.

Therapeutic category	Value sales (share)
ACE Inhibitors	$1,000m
Calcium channel blockers	$2,000m
Beta blockers	$1,000m
Diuretics	$400m

It looks as though the (then) 'modern therapies' (ACE inhibitors and calcium channel blockers) have almost achieved market saturation. But value sales can be decomposed into:

volume sales x price

This gives the following picture:

US ANTI-HYPERTENSIVES MARKET 1990: VOLUME, PRICE AND VALUE

Therapeutic category	Volume sales (standard units)	Average price (per standard unit)	Value sales
ACE Inhibitors	2,000m	$0.5	$1,000m
CBBs	3,000m	$0.6	$2,000m
Beta blockers	3,000m	$0.3	$1,000m
Diuretics	5,000m	$0.1	$400m

Immediately you can see that there is a huge low-priced beta-blocker and diuretics markets waiting to be superceded. Already this decomposed approach is pointing us towards the assumptions that matter and making market understanding and accurate forecasts much more likely.

A decomposed approach also encourages us to start with the general and proceed to the specific.

For example, a forecast using data from up to 1957 forecast attempted to predict the future sales of transistors by considering only the past trend in transistor sales. The forecast was for between 6 billion and 690 billion units per year[22].

But, taking a more general perspective, transistors were competing with vacuum tubes in the broader semi-conductors market. This market had a far lower and more predictable growth rate of around 10% per year. If one assumed that this growth would continue and that transistors would increase their share from a starting point of 6% to , the mid-point of the range of possible shares (from 6% to 100%) i.e. 53%, then a forecast of 700 million would result[5]. The actual production in 1966 was 850 million.

So, when we proceed to the specific techniques of pharmaceutical sales forecasting, you will see that we start with patient numbers (general), then proceed to estimate what proportion of these will be treated by our therapeutic category (more specific) and finally what market share our product will command in that therapeutic category (very specific).

Principle 2: Be Conservative

The principle of conservatism in forecasting has been defined by the American forecasting guru, Scott Armstrong[5]: 'to the extent that you are uncertain about the evidence, you should forecast small changes from the current situation'

We now consider some examples of how conservatism helps in forecasting

Futurology should be tempered

We have already encountered one situation where conservatism would have helped: futurology. We saw in the introduction that futurologists predicting radical change in the health care environment have failed miserably. In fact, better forecasts often result from predicting no change. Despite all the apocalyptic visions of 'future shock' and 'turbulent times ahead', things don't change as much as you might expect.

In 1959, the New York Times asked three American historians to predict what the United States would be like in 1970, just over a decade in the future. Two of the historians indulged in flights of science fiction fantasy. Their predictions were hopelessly inaccurate. The most successful of the three, Crane Brinton, summed up his view of the future like this:

'I should expect life in the United States then to be substantially what it is now. I suppose this opinion will not be shared by most of my colleagues, but to me, at least, it is a view dictated by the course of human history,'[11]

Shockingly, there is no future shock. William Ascher conducted a huge survey of past forecasts and concluded that: 'The hypothesis of accelerating change is just not supported by the empirical evidence of past forecasts. Most...forecasts...overshot their targets by a mile.'[7]

§

During the first half of the 1990's, conference after conference and report after report forecast a 'black hole' where pharmaceutical sales would be decimated and pharmaceutical field forces rendered a thing of the past. The industry braced itself. Pharmaceutical stocks nose-dived. Field forces started to be downsized.

Finally, people had to start to accept that the facts just did not tally with this apocalyptic forecast.

In October of 1997, Robert Merold, general manager of IMS America's healthcare division told an investment conference in New York that: 'Contrary to all forecasts, managed care is actually a tremendous help to the pharmaceutical industry'[10].

The reason, it turns out is that managed care encourages larger prescriptions of what tend to be branded, more novel drugs. The reason is that managed care meant that more people were having a third party pay for their drug rather than having to pay themselves. As Mr Merold put it: 'When it's not their money and there is only a small co-payment, a person will usually say "I'll take the brand"'.

The fact is that you could have produced a more accurate forecast of the impact of managed care by simply assuming little or no change from the *status quo ante*.

So, why, in the face of all the evidence, do forecasters make such radical forecasts? At least part of the answer lies in the fact that it suites forecasters to hype up the prospects for the market they are forecasting. Would you buy a report on a new pharmaceutical market whose headline read 'This market is expected to deliver modest growth and to remain of marginal significance to the industry'?

Indeed, the research director of one forecasting institution is on record as saying, 'The higher my [forecast] numbers, the more reports I can sell'[23].

Conservatism means you should not be too optimistic with your sales forecasts

So, most forecasts overshoot the mark. This is particularly true when it comes to forecasting the sales of our own products. One reason that sales forecasts tend to be optimistic is that the marketing people who make them are optimistic and aggressive individuals. These are often useful traits in marketing. But not when it comes to making accurate forecasts.

Marketing agency chiefs Kevin Clancy and Robert Schulman have been helping marketers come up with forecasts for decades. They observe that, 'marketing executives routinely ask us if there aren't circumstances that would lead us to adjust simulated test market forecasts upwards. We have *never* been asked to revise a sales forecast downwards.'[24]

§

I once attended a large international asthma conference. During discussions with marketing executives from the major asthma companies, (using tactics of which I am not proud) I got ballpark estimates of their future market share forecasts for their anti-inflammatory asthma products. Totalling all the forecasts gave a combined market share of nearly 200%. Clearly somebody, if not everybody is going to be disappointed.

Conservatism means you should be suspicious of trends

Conservatism also means that you should be suspicious of trends. Nobel laureate, Kenneth Arrow suggests that the earthquake insurance paradox applies to forecasting. The more years pass since the last earthquake, the more people reduce their earthquake insurance. But, they *should* do the opposite. A similar phenomenon occurs with forecasting. The faster a market grows, the more people ramp up their forecasts. Often, they should do the opposite.

You will see later – when we look at extrapolation forecasts in depth – that it is generally possible to improve their accuracy by damping down the effect of a trend. In other words by being *conservative*.

Principle 3: Keep it Simple

We know that it is complexity that limits the growth of big businesses. We know that in business we should 'keep it simple'. But, when it comes to forecasting, we often tend not to. Why is this?

Things get complicated because experts are a solution waiting for a problem

Part of the answer, at least, lies in the fact that we often look to experts to help us with our forecasting. And experts are a solution waiting for a problem. We all tend to see the world through the lens of our own particular knowledge and expertise.

> In a classic 1958 study, Dearborn and Simon[25] presented a group of executives with a long a complex case study. They then asked the executives what the root of the problem was. Five out of six sales executives saw it as a sales problem. All four production executives saw it as a production problem.

So, asking an expert how to analyse a problem is akin to asking a barber if you need a haircut. If you ask an agency that specialises in discrete choice conjoint analysis for help with your forecast, they will recommend a discrete choice conjoint analysis. If you ask an agency that specialises in complex mathematical extrapolation models, like Box-Jenkins (more on which later), they will recommend a complex mathematical extrapolation model.

There is good evidence that just this phenomenon occurs with forecasting experts.

> Forecasters' livelihoods depend upon their models being so complex that only they can understand and operate them. A survey of such experts, found that 72% agreed that complexity enhanced accuracy and only 9% disagreed. The experts who believed in complexity did so with great conviction. The average confidence level was 4.0 on a five-point scale.
>
> §
>
> I observed the same phenomenon recently when I talked on the value of simplicity in forecasting at a major pharmaceutical market research conference. Most of the audience agreed with the evidence that complex models offer no advantages – except the people from agencies that sell the complicated models.

But complicated forecasts are no more accurate than simple forecasts

Perhaps because the world out there is complicated, we feel that a forecasting model has to be complicated to stand any chance of mimicking the real world. Surprisingly, it doesn't work like that. Complex systems can be modelled as well with simple models as with complex models.

There is a branch of science concerned with the study of complex systems (known as complexity theory). The pre-eminent figure is Per Bak, Professor of Theoretical Physics at the Niels Bohr Institute in Copenhagen and discoverer of 'self organised criticality'. This is what Bak says about modelling complex systems in general[26]: 'Insight seldom arises from complex messy modelling (sic), but more often from gross simplifications.'

A graphic illustration of Bak's point comes from the most complex system that there is to model: an entire economy. Economists have produced some staggeringly complex models of the economy. In some cases these have – in an attempt to capture reality – contained hundreds of variables. Amazingly, these complex models have proven no more accurate than drastically simpler models using just a handful of key variables

A 1992 review of the accuracy of economic models[27] was a stark demonstration that adding more and more complexity does nothing to help accuracy in forecasting – and may actually have a negative effect. Models with just a handful of variables are likely to be as good *or better* than models with thousands of variables.

Later in this book, we will review the impact of complexity on each of the different techniques for forecasting pharmaceutical sales. Again and again you will see that the evidence points to the same conclusion: there is no gain in accuracy from making forecasting models overly complicated. Indeed, sometimes there are losses in accuracy.

And there are major benefits to keeping things simple

Not only is there no loss in accuracy if you keep things simple, there are many profound advantages.

Firstly, simple models are user friendly: they are cheap, fast to build and easy to use.

Glen Urban, Professor of Management at M.I.T and one of the high priests of management science says that: 'Although there are sophisticated management science models, very few complex ones have achieved continuing use.'[28]

Professor Urban cites four reasons why models run into trouble: they are hard to understand, are supported by limited data, cost a lot and take a long time to develop.

§

According to John Little, Professor of Management at M.I.T., models have to be: 'Quick, quick, quick. If you can answer people's questions right away, you will affect their thinking. If you cannot, they will make their decisions without you and go on to something else.'[29]

Secondly, if you keep things simple you are less likely to make mistakes.
You are less likely to make accidental mistakes

Armstrong's laws for using econometric models are: (1) keep it simple and (2) don't make mistakes. The idea is that if you obey rule 1, rule 2 becomes easier to follow[5].

And, you are less likely to make the mistake of believing charlatans who shelter behind the sophistry of complex models.

Forecasting authority, Stephen Schnaars advises us to, 'Be especially suspicious of forecasts made by forecasters enamoured by statistical jargon. A good rule of thumb is to discount estimates in direct proportion to the number of times they mention "parameters", "estimation procedures", and "optimization techniques"[11].

The classic Doctor Fox lectures remind us of just how susceptible we are to phoney 'experts'[30].

> Dr. Fox was an actor. A distinguished looking and authoritative sounding actor. Like most actors, he knew absolutely nothing about 'Mathematical Game Theory as Applied to Physician Education'. And yet - armed with a fictitious impressive looking resume - this is the very topic he lectured on to 55 psychologists, educators, psychiatrists, social workers and administrators. The talk lasted a full hour. What is more the entirely ignorant Dr Fox took half an hour's questions on this subject about which he knew absolutely nothing. His entire performance consisted of double talk, meaningless words, false logic, contradictory statements, irrelevant humour and meaningless references to unrelated topics.
>
> And yet, according to a questionnaire administered at the end of each session, the audience found the lecture to be clear and stimulating. They held Dr. Fox in high regard. No one realised that the whole thing was nonsense.
>
> §
>
> A follow-up study[31] found that researchers who write in a style that is difficult to understand are more highly regarded than their peers who foolishly adopt a simple and lucid style.

If you stick to simple models, you are less likely to be fooled by this sort of thing.

Thirdly, if you keep your models simple, you can concentrate on the key determinant of forecasts' accuracy: the assumptions you make.

> William Ascher[7] studied many forecasts and looked at where the inaccuracies came from. He concluded that mistaken assumptions were a much bigger problem than faulty models.

Lastly, and perhaps most importantly, if you keep your models simple, you will have the time, money and energy to look at several different models, to look at our problem from a variety of angles. Which brings us to another vital principle in forecasting...

Principle 4: Look at the Problem from Many Angles

The realisation that forecasting in complicated situations can be improved by looking at the problem from a variety of angles is credited not to a businessperson or even an economist, but a biologist. Richard Levins was a population biologist. He realised that an ecosystem (like a market place) is so complicated that there is no prospect of building a full model of it. Levins championed the idea of looking at a number of simple, partial models. He once famously said that 'our truth is the intersection of independent lies'[32].

Since then, studies have shown again and again – almost without fail – that combinations of different forecasts are more accurate than individual forecasts alone.

> After an extensive review of the evidence, Stephen Schnaars has concluded that, 'One of the most prominent findings of the forecasting literature is that multiple methods, combinations of forecasts, and averages of estimates are superior to forecasts based on only a single method. When given the choice, breadth of analysis almost always wins

over depth of study. Multiple methods almost universally yield more accurate forecasts than a single forecasting model, no matter how elegant the model may be. This finding has held true for all types of forecasting. It is especially true for growth market forecasting.'[11]

It turns out that forecasting is like trying to make out the shape of a 3-dimensional shape from 2-dimensional pictures. A combination of different 2-D views is more likely to give you an accurate idea of what the real 3-dimensional shape is.

Two 2-dimensional views might give you the following pictures:

WHAT DO YOU THINK YOU ARE LOOKING AT?

Taken individually, you might think that you are looking at a diamond and a sphere. Taken together, you might infer that you are looking at one of these:

TWO PERSPECTIVES COMBINED MAKE IT CLEAR

You can only get to the real truth by combining more than one view.

What types of forecasts to combine?

Intuitively, it makes sense to combine forecasts that use different approaches and different data. That way you benefit from taking into account all the different factors that could affect the forecast. And, there is powerful evidence that this approach works.

Scott Armstrong[5] reviewed eight studies that had combined two methods and concluded that: 'Combining is a powerful strategy! Combinations of two methods reduced the error by over 6%. It never hurt accuracy.' Armstrong opined that: 'Combinations of forecasts from three methods are expected to yield even further improvements.' Of the two studies he found, the average improvement was even greater at 9% - but one had boosted accuracy by 18%, while the other had not affected accuracy.

What weight should you give to each of the combined forecasts?

If forecasts are to be combined, what weight should be given to each? The evidence here harks back to the preceding principle: keep things simple. Armstrong[33], in reviewing the evidence, concludes that, 'Research to date suggests that equal weighting of the various forecasts is sufficient. A useful approach would be to take an average of the cheapest and most easily understood methods.'

A note of caution

Don't expect your forecasting or market research consultants to agree with this principle. I recently gave a talk where I reviewed some of the evidence presented here that a broad perspective (several simple forecasts combined) beats a depth perspective (one complex, costly methodology). Pharmaceutical marketing people bought the concept totally (the evidence is overwhelming). Agency people, who sell the big expensive models, viewed me as a heretic. But when they can charge six figure sums for one of their models, I can understand their concerns.

Principle 5: Use scientific tools scientifically

The essence of the scientific method

Human kind's greatest piece of practical philosophy - perhaps its only piece of practical philosophy – is the scientific method. The essence of the scientific method is that *the theory precedes the data* (a so-called *a priori* approach). Then the theory stands or falls on whether the data support it. The advent of cheap computing power and complex statistical packages has increasingly meant that, in market research and forecasting, the scientific method has been stood on its head. Often today, the data precedes the theory (a so-called *a posteriori* approach). This can be a recipe for disaster. Statistics are scientific tools and the key to using them properly is simply to apply the scientific method to your research.

The scientific method has evolved over the last four hundred years. The first man to propose a scientific method was Francis Bacon. Bacon was a lawyer who liked a challenge. So, he set out in his spare time to catalogue all existing knowledge. In his professional role, he liked to personally supervise the torture of his victims. Perhaps this is what inspired his view of science for Bacon believed that if you torture enough data, the truth will emerge. (This is the process of induction whereby you collect more and more facts until eventually the truth becomes evident.) Towards the end of his life, Bacon decided to do some science rather that just writing about it. He made no useful discoveries. (In fact, he caught a cold whilst trying to freeze a chicken in the snow and died.).

More than two centuries later, this is what a much more successful scientist – Charles Darwin - had to say about Bacon's view of science: '[you] might as well go into a gravel-pit and count the pebbles and describe the colours'. and 'How odd it is that anyone should not see that all observation must be for or against some view if it is to be of any service'.

Darwin was summing up the essence of the scientific method, that the theory should precede the data. This is as true for forecasting as it is for high science. Here's an example of why. Let's put the theory first. Lets suppose that you have a theory that doctors with blue eyes are more likely to prescribe ACE inhibitors. You could conduct a survey collecting eye colour and ACE prescribing data. You could then statistically analyse the correlation. If there is no correlation it is very unlikely that you will see a statistically significant correlation.

But what if you put the facts before the theory. What if you go out and collect data on a hundred physical characteristics of doctors alongside their ACE prescribing habits. You could collect data on weight, height, hair colour, whether they have a hairy chest and so on. Then, if you look for statistically significant correlations between each of these and ACE prescribing you will, on average, find 5 'statistically significant' correlations *by chance.* You might then start using these 'relationships' to make forecasts.

David Raup - a statistical palaeontologist of all things - provides another great example of how correlations that are found from extensive data-dredging are highly suspect[34]:

'The fatal flaw in this logic is that testing cannot be adjusted for the fact that we tried many traits before finding a promising one. Remember that one out of every twenty completely random sprinklings will, on average, pass our test if odds of twenty to one are considered acceptable - as is common in scientific research. Because it is virtually impossible to keep track of the number of traits we have considered - many were discarded at a glance - we cannot evaluate the test results for any one trait.'

Raup goes on to demonstrate how evidence for a bizarre theory can be uncovered and given credence by data-dredging:

'Research has shown that people are strongly attracted to cities with names starting in the second half of the alphabet ... the seven most populous metropolitan areas are (in descending order):

Tokyo-Yokohama
New York
Mexico City
Osaka-Kobe-Kyoto
Sao Paulo
Seoul
Moscow

Note that all of these names start with the M-Z range, virtually the second half of the alphabet. ... It could be argued that this near-perfect correlation is an accident of random sprinkling of populations and city names. It is also possible that most cities in the world have initial letters late in the alphabet. To test this hypothesis, a control sample was taken from the same source. The next seven most populous metropolitan areas are (in order):

Calcutta
Buenos Aires
London
Bombay
Los Angeles
Cairo
Rio de Janeiro

With one exception of Rio de Janeiro, all have initial letters drawn from the A-L part of the alphabet...The statistical likelihood that this was caused by chance alone is so small that rejection of a hypothesis of randomness is routine. Cause and effect are clearly indicated ...

See how easy it is to establish a case for selectivity?'

How to avoid exploratory research

These sorts of nonsense relationships are increasingly uncovered in forecasting. This is because modern computer programmes are so powerful that they can make a lot of sense and see quite plausible patterns in noise. As long ago as 1972 Hillel Einhorn was warning that 'proceeding via a "dustbowl" empiricism is dangerous at worst and foolish at best"[35]. In his paper entitled 'Alchemy in the Behavioral Sciences', Einhorn relates example after example of powerful computer based statistical packages seeing patterns in random data or nonsense data. High on the list of offending techniques are:

- Automatic Interaction Detection (AID)
- Multiple Regression (particularly step-wise regression)
- Factor Analysis and
- Multidimensional Scaling (MDS)

Einhorn concludes by warning that, 'Just as the ancient alchemists were not successful in turning base metal into gold, the modern researcher cannot rely on the "computer" to turn his data into meaningful and valuable scientific information.'

Another way to see spurious relationships is to build a forecasting model with many 'parameters' (forecasting jargon for unknown constants) and then use some sort of optimisation technique to find the best fit with past data. The fact is that with enough 'parameters' in the model, you can always find a reasonably good fit with *past* data. (The problem is that it is highly likely that you have found patterns in noise and that your model will be hopeless at forecasting the future.)

Following a detailed review of the evidence on such *a posteriori* approaches to forecasting, Professor Scott Armstrong [5] drew the following conclusion: 'A good rule to follow about *a posteriori* analysis is this: Avoid it!'

Forecasting and market research agencies have not heeded such warnings. Presumably, this is because they make so much money out of *a posteriori* methodologies (and the big surveys that they often entail).

Exploratory research has a role. But it is in generating ideas, not in drawing conclusions.

Forecast uncertainty is always uncertain

Obviously, when you make forecasts, you would like to have some idea of how accurate they are likely to be. Because we use statistics to describe the accuracy of forecasts,it is easy to be blinded by science and to get a dangerously inaccurate idea of how accurate your forecasts are.

There are two things to bear in mind. First, if you are using objective data you can see how well your forecasting model fits past data. But the fit of past data and the fit of future data are two completely different things – especially if you have searched for the best fit to the past data. (See above!) There are times when the fit to past data is a reasonable guide to expected future forecast accuracy – and we will cover these – but this is not the norm.

Second, if you use judgements as the basis of your forecasts, judges consistently underestimate the uncertainty in a forecast.

In 1972, Ross McDonald examined fifteen expert estimates of how far the Sun is from the Earth. The estimates spanned a period from 1895 to 1961. Each later (and generally more accurate) estimate was outside the certainty limits set by his immediate predecessor. McDonald concluded that a useful rule of thumb is to obtain the best estimates of error that you can from independent sources and then multiply by three.

Benjamin Franklin used to make experts summarise the arguments *against* their predictions as well as those *for* to try to get people to think through the uncertainties.

Benjamin Franklin's method might help, but what ever you do, judges are poor judges of the accuracy of their own forecasts.

Nevertheless, such estimates are routinely fed into sophisticated Monte Carlo simulation programs.

Don't gamble on Monte Carlo simulations

Monte Carlo simulation works like this. Let us assume that that you think you can judge patient numbers, therapy class penetration of patients and your product's share of therapy class like this:

AN EXAMPLE OF A RANGE OF FORECASTS WITH PROBABILITIES

	(a) < 5% probability no lower than…	(b) Most likely forecast	(c) < 5% probability no higher than…
Patient numbers	10 million	20 million	30 million
Therapy class penetration	5%	20%	35%
Your products share of class	2%	5%	10%

If you multiply the highest estimates (column c) for patients, category share and product share to give you an upper estimate you get 1 million patients treated (30 million x 35% x 10%). And a lower limit (column a) of 0.01 million. This spread is so huge that the forecast is all but useless – the upper limit is 100 times the lower limit.

But what are the chances of one of these extreme values occurring? The answer is: 5%x5%x5% = 0.01%. This is so unlikely as to be practically impossible. Therefore, you need a way of combining the above estimates to give a useful upper and lower estimate that are within the bounds of reasonable probability (as were the estimates that you started off with).

Monte Carlo simulation achieves this by assuming that your estimates of patient number, class share and product share have a certain probability distribution. This could be, for example, a normal distribution in which case your upper and lower estimates are for about 2 standard deviations from the most likely forecast. Now a Monte Carlo simulation would perform your product sales calculation (sales = patients x class share x product share) hundreds of times. The value for each variable is chosen by a random number generator but such that the probability of any value is proportional to the probability distribution that you have assumed. So, patient numbers close to 20 million will be much more common than patient numbers close to 10 million. Then, when these hundreds of iterations have been run, the distribution (relative frequency) of the results are displayed.

In this example, the results of a Monte Carlo simulation looked like this:

RESULTS OF MONTE CARLO SIMULATION

Probability...	Of sales being above...
5%	0.4million
25%	0.25million
50%	0.2 million
75%	0.15 million
95%	0.05million

There is now just an eightfold difference between the upper and lower forecasts. And, if you are happy to live with forecasts that have a 50-50 chance of being right the upper forecast is less than twice the lower forecast.

The result is an impressive looking estimate of possible outcomes each with probability figures attached. The whole thing is, unfortunately, entirely spurious. The probability estimates entered into the simulation are generally from experts. We have already seen that experts estimates of the uncertainty in forecasts are so bad as to be meaningless. So, therefore, is the sophisticated looking output.

Don't make errors measuring errors

On the subject of forecast error, it is helpful to think about the best way to measure forecast error.

One figure that is often quoted is R^2. This statistic (known as the coefficient of determination) is a measure of how closely two variables are correlated. In other words the degree to which when one goes up, the other one does too. It is in theory possible to have a forecast and an actual *totally* correlated ($R^2 = 100\%$) and yet wildly different in value. For example:

PERFECT R² BUT POOR FORECAST

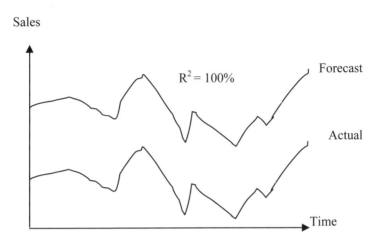

Therefore, R^2 is not a good measure of forecast accuracy.

A simpler and more meaningful figure is the absolute percentage error. So, if the actual is 50 units and the forecast is 55 units, the absolute percentage error is 10%. (The forecast is out by 5 units and 5 units is 10% of the actual figure of 50 units.)

When the accuracies of a number of forecasts (say for different years or products) need to be combined, the simplest measure of accuracy is the mean absolute percentage error (MAPE). This simple and intuitive measure is the one used most often in this book.

Sometimes, however, when errors get quite large, it is necessary to complicate things a little and to derive an adjusted mean absolute percentage error (aMAPE). This is because an unadjusted MAPE favours low forecasts over high forecasts when errors get quite big. The details of why this is and how to adjust an MAPE follow for those who are interested.

The reason that unadjusted MAPEs favour low forecasts when errors get large is as follows. Say our actual is 50 units. A forecast that is too high by 50 units and a forecast that is too low by 50 units both have an MAPE of 100%. But, the low forecast is far worse. The actual is infinitely greater than the forecast. Whereas, the actual is only 50% less than the high forecast.

So, another measure, the adjusted absolute percentage error can be used. The adjusted absolute error adjusts so that low forecasts are not favoured. This is done by expressing the error as a percentage of the mid point between the actual and the error.

So, using the above example, if our actual is 50 units a forecast 50 units above this (i.e. 100 units) has an adjusted absolute percentage error of 50 units/75 units = 67%. An error 50 units below this actual (i.e. 0 units) has an adjusted absolute percentage error or 50 units/25 units = 200%.

Now the low forecast is rightly seen as being more inaccurate than the high forecast. (This demonstrates a point about adjusted percentage errors: the worst possible error in either direction is 200%. So, forecasts with adjusted mean absolute percentage errors approaching 200% are utterly useless.)

Provided errors are relatively small, it does not make much difference whether the absolute percentage error is adjusted or not as both give approximately the same figure. Incidentally, if errors are normally distributed, the MAPE and the aMAPE both tend to be somewhat larger than one standard deviation. In other words, something in the order of three-quarters of forecasts will be within the MAPE or aMAPE.

What level of error might you have to be prepared for?

In 1984, John Mentzer and James Cox[36] surveyed the size in the errors (mean absolute percentage error) in sales forecasts from 160 US corporations. The results were:

ERRORS IN A SURVEY OF US SALES FORECASTS

Level	Forecast horizon		
	< 3 months	3-24 months	>24 months
Industry	8	11	15
Corporate	7	11	18
Product group	10	15	20
Product line	11	16	20
Product	16	21	26

This survey makes an important point: the lower the level of detail, the more inaccurate the forecast. So, product presentation forecasts will be less accurate than total product forecasts; country by country forecasts will be less accurate than global forecasts. The survey was, however, mainly concerned with established products. It does suggest a level of accuracy that is unrealistic where new product categories are concerned. In my experience, the levels of accuracy that you can expect are shown in the table on the following page. (As some of the error levels are big, I use adjusted mean absolute percentage errors.)

(* The pharmaceutical industry is in the same position as the auto industry when it comes to test marketing. To test market a car you would need, say, 1,000 cars. That requires you to build a full production line. Once the sunk cost is incurred, you might as well launch the thing for real. It is the same with pharmaceuticals. You have to develop and register a drug before you can test market it.)

EXPECTED ERRORS FROM DIFFERENT FORECAST TYPES

Adjusted MAPE	Usefulness	Examples for forecasts several years out
100-200%	Hopelessly inaccurate	Futurologists
50-100%	Better than nothing, but treat with extreme caution	Experts Diffusion models to forecast new therapeutic category sales when there is no historic sales data
25-50%	Useful ranging shot	Single bootstrapping or econometric models to predict market shares in markets with established dynamics Diffusion models to forecast new therapeutic category sales when there is limited historic sales data
12.5-25%	Very helpful tool	Basket of bootstrapping and econometric models to estimate market share in market with established dynamics Diffusion models with substantial historic data
12.5%	Nirvana!!	Test marketing* Extrapolation of stable patient population trends

Principle 6: Use Techniques Proven to Work in the Real World

It seems obvious that we should use techniques that work. Unfortunately, most forecasting techniques have not been shown to work in the real world. And, even when a technique is said to be 'valid', you cannot assume that this means that it works in the real world. To appreciate why, it is worth reviewing the concept of validity.

What validity and reliability mean

Validity means that something does what it is supposed to do 'truthfully'. A valid measure measures what it is supposed to measure. A valid forecasting technique forecasts what it is supposed to forecast reasonably accurately. (Incidentally, reliability, which is often talked about alongside validity, means that something gives the same answer when used in the same situation repeatedly.)

Unfortunately, when you read that something is 'valid' you cannot take it to mean that it has been shown to be useful at forecasting in the real world. This is because academics complicate things by recognising three different types of validity. It is important to see through these different types of validity, otherwise, you can be lead to believe that you are using a model that has been shown to be useful at making real world forecasts when it has not.

Face validity means that 'experts' agree that something is reasonable 'on the *face* of it'. But in areas where there is little empirical data, an expert's guess is no better than yours or mine. Face validity is a very weak measure of the value of anything.

Construct - or conceptual - validity means that an operational measure measures what it is supposed to measure. This is typically determined by checking that the measure corresponds to other operational measures of the same concept. Later, we will see that it usually makes little difference in forecasting which operational measure you choose. So, this is usually not a very helpful measure.

Predictive - or forecast - validity means that something is useful in making forecasts. This is a most useful measure of the value of something. But beware. Researchers often test the 'predictive validity' of a technique 'in the laboratory'. For example, they will get some doctors to rank product profiles and then come up with a conjoint model to describe the decision making process that the doctors have used. They will test the conjoint model on some other product profiles that the doctors have ranked and see how well they can forecast their choices. (This is often referred to as a 'hold-out' test, because some of the doctors rankings are held out until after the model has been made and then used to test it.) But all such a test does is to tell us how good the conjoint model is at predicting what doctors *say* they will do in a *paper and pencil exercise*.

What you want – and what this book aims to distil out – are the techniques that have predictive validity in the real world.

An introduction to the concept of a forecasting model

As you will see, most of the techniques that have predictive validity in the real world are forecasting models. So, it would be useful to start by being clear on what a model is.

A model is a simplified representation of the real world. Professor John Little says that a model is 'a preconceived idea of how the world works *and therefore of what is interesting and worthwhile'*[29].

There are different types of models: there are verbal models (that explain things in words), graphical models (that explain things in picture or diagram form and there are mathematical models (that explain things with numbers).

For example, the most famous forecasting model of all is the Bass Model. It allows us to forecast how quickly new product categories are adopted. (You will cover this in much greater detail later, so don't be concerned if what follows is unclear.) The Bass Model can be represented:

In words:

'Initially, a few innovators try and then adopt a new type of product. These innovators are then imitated and more people adopt the product. As more and more people adopt, there are more and more people to imitate. So, the rate of adoption accelerates. Eventually, the pool of users starts to be saturated and so the adoption rate levels off.

Graphically:

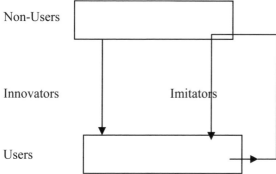

Or mathematically:

Rate of adoption = (rate of innovation) + (rate of imitation)
Rate of innovation = (proportion of non-users) x (a constant)
Rate of imitation = (proportion of non-users) x (proportion of users) x (a constant)

We will be representing models in all these forms. Verbal and graphical models will allow you to understand the underlying concepts. But our ultimate goal is to describe mathematical models, because mathematical models produce numerical forecasts that you can test and use.

Also, mathematical models are the only type of model that allows you (or anybody else) to make the forecast in exactly the same way each time. So, when you have uncovered a good model, you can keep using it.

But the trouble with most forecasting models is managers *don't* use them. According to John Little, Professor of Management at MIT, 'The big problem with management science models is that managers practically never use them.'[37]

He is right, the sales forecasts adopted for most pharmaceutical companies budgets are estimated primarily by judgement.

Gert Assmus, professor of business administration at the Amos Tuck School at Dartmouth, thinks there is a solution. He believes that a model is more acceptable if it is: applicable earlier in development, includes crucial marketing decision variables, uses existing data and experience and can be trusted by marketing management[38].

A key purpose of this book is to present you with simple models that meet all of Professor Assmus's criteria for acceptable models. It is then up to you whether you use them.

Chapter 2

Chapter 2: Informal ("subjective") forecasts

In judgement be ye not too confident
Dante

Before we start to look at forecasting models in depth, we should first deal with the alternative way of doing forecasts. This is to make informal or subjective forecasts. We now review when it is best to make informal forecasts and how to make the best such forecasts.

Informal ("subjective") forecasts vs. models

Another term for a forecasting model would be an 'objective forecast'. They are called 'objective' because they use well specified techniques that can be replicated by other forecasters. So, objective measures of the accuracy of these techniques can be obtained. (Incidentally, don't confuse the type of method with the type of data. An objective *method* may use either objective data - like sales volumes - and/or subjective data - like product preferences.)

Subjective methods on the other hand are those where the method of analysis has not been well specified. Subjective methods are also called informal, experience based or intuitive methods. Most forecasts are made using subjective methods. Think about your experience: most sales forecasts in pharmaceuticals involve managers looking at what a product and its competitors have sold in the past and then estimating future sales. Furthermore, the more important the forecast, the greater the tendency to use subjective methods[5]. Again, think of your own experience. Even if objective methods are used to make initial forecasts, those forecasts will be tweaked again and again by senior managers during the budgeting process. And all the tweaking is purely subjective.

So, the first and most important decision you have to make in deciding how to make your forecast is whether to use subjective (informal) methods or objective methods (models).

A general review of the forecasting literature leads inexorably to the following general conclusion: Informal forecasts are best when there is little change ahead and little objective data available. Models are best when there is change ahead and where there is plenty of objective data to feed a model. (Because there will tend to be more change in the long term than the short term, this implies – rightly – that models are better for long term forecasts.)

When there are changes ahead and when there is data that you can use, subjective forecasts are relatively poor.

One interesting study that looked at the relative accuracy of judgement (subjective), extrapolation (objective) and econometric (objective) methods over varying time frames in the US air travel market[39].

Expert forecasts by the Federal Aviation Authority (FAA) were compared with a very simple extrapolation model, which assumed a constant percentage growth, and an econometric model. (We will define exactly what is meant by an extrapolation model and an econometric model later, but they are key types of forecasting models.) The results were as follows:

INFORMAL FORECASTS VS. FORECASTING MODELS IN THE AIR TRAVEL INDUSTRY

Forecast horizon (years)	Number of forecasts	Error (mean absolute percentage error)		
		Informal forecast	Extrapolation model	Causal model
1	6	6.8	5.7	4.2
2	5	15.6	12.7	6.8
3	4	25.1	17.4	7.3
4	3	34.1	22.5	9.8
5	2	42.1	27.5	6.2
6	1	45.0	29.9	0.7
Average	21	28.1	19.3	5.8

There is plenty of objective data in the air travel industry (just like in the pharmaceutical industry). So, as predicted, objective forecasts are best. Furthermore, they are much better over longer time periods when change is necessarily greater.

A review of the forecasting literature [5] confirms that informal forecasts are better where there is little objective data (you don't have much choice) but that otherwise, forecasting models tend to be better. (This review was undertaken by, Scott Armstrong, Professor of Marketing at the Warton School of Management in Philadelphia. Professor Armstrong has done more than any other academic – and indeed possibly as much as all other academics put together – to tease out the evidence for which forecasting approaches work best.)

THE RELATIVE PERFORMANCE OF INFORMAL FORECASTS AND MODELS

		Few objective data	Many objective data
Small change	Informal forecasts better	17	1
	No difference	3	2
	Models better	7	2
Large change	Informal forecasts better	1	1
	No difference	1	1
	Models better	0	3

As long as there is data, models generally perform better. Models also tend to perform better for pharmaceutical forecasting

I once – in collaboration with a number of country managers – produced a forecasting model to predict sales country by country for a large respiratory compound. Our company was experiencing severe problems and needed a sales turn around to survive. I kept a record of the model's forecasts and the forecasts that were actually produced at the end of a highly informal (subjective) budgeting process.

The relative accuracy of the forecasts were:

**INFORMAL VS. MODEL FORECAST ERRORS (MAPES) IN A
PHARMACEUTICAL COMPANY**

	Informal forecast	Model
Product already launched	21.8%	4.5%
Product being launched in year of forecast	131%	22.9%

This illustrates a big problem with informal forecasts. Because they are a one-off, there is no record of their use in other situations to give you a steer on how valid and reliable they are. Therefore, in a difficult and politically charged planning process, there is no real anchor to keep people in touch with reality. People (with the best of intentions) tend to produce wish driven forecasts rather than reality driven forecasts.

Sometimes of course, people don't have the best of intentions. Informal forecasts produced to appraise business development opportunities (licensing deals or acquisitions) can be outrageously unrealistic. Sometimes both parties (the buyer and the seller) are unrealistically optimistic. The seller wants the best price and the acquiring management wants a bigger empire. If you are interested in the good of the shareholders, informal forecasts of business development opportunities should be banned!

The conclusion: if you have the data (and pharmaceuticals is a very data rich industry) use models to forecast.

What about starting with models and then adding subjective input?

Often – as already noted - people start the forecasting process with a model and then 'tweak' the forecast using their judgement. Evidence from people who learn the hard way how reliable forecasts are suggests that the more you tweak, the more inaccurate your forecasts become.

Auditors, who have to make professional judgements on the adequacy of companies' forecasting systems have been shown to place less confidence in forecasts where large revisions were made between the initial and the final forecasts[40].
Weather forecasters take the same view[41].

And, in business forecasting, the evidence points in the same direction.

In 1956, Lydia Strong[42] published the results of a survey in *Management Review* entitled 'Sales Forecasting Comes of Age'. Apparently it didn't because the basic error that she highlighted is still rampant today. Strong surveyed managers at the American Marketing Association conference on sales forecasting. She looked at the extent to which they tempered forecasts with judgement and at the accuracy of their most recent one-year forecasts. The results speak for themselves:

EFFECT OF JUDGEMENT ON FORECAST ACCURACY

Use of judgement	MAPE
Don't use judgement	6.8%
Used judgement	8.5%
Used mainly judgement	9.6%

So, judgement forecasts are indicated where there is little objective data and therefore, a model cannot be built. Also experts are fairly good at assessing the current situation. We now review the evidence for how best to obtain informal (judgement) forecasts using our six principles of good forecasting as a framework.

How the "six principles" apply to informal forecasts

Principle 1: Break the Problem Down

The way questions are framed to the people who are going to make your judgements has a profound impact on the replies. Generally, the more general the question, the more general and vague the answer. The more specific and decomposed the question, the more specific and realistic the answer.

> For example, when US citizens were asked this question: 'Do you believe in freedom of speech?', 96% answered 'yes'. But when they were asked the more specific question, 'Do you believe in freedom of speech to the extent of allowing radicals to hold meetings and express their views to the community?', only22% answered 'yes'[43].

And the more you can break the problem down for your subjects and focus them on the key specific issues, the better.

> Linda Dudycha and James Naylor performed a fascinating experiment back in 1966[44]. They created a virtual system in which two predictor variables were imperfectly correlated to an outcome. Subjects were shown the value of the one of the predictors in one study and then of both predictors in a second study. The degree of correlation between the predictors and the outcome was varied between different subjects. Reassuringly, the better the correlation between the first predictor and the outcome, the better subjects got at predicting the outcome. But when the second variable was added, things got interesting. This second variable helped when the first predictor was a poor predictor but hindered when the first predictor was good. And the second variable hindered even if it was a very accurate predictor of outcome. The moral is, if you are making subjective judgements and you have one good predictor that you can more or less rely on, stick with it.

Principle 2: Be Conservative

Biases in judgement forecasts can come from a number of sources. A lack of conservatism, encouraged by ill-founded optimism is often the reason.

The problem of well intentioned optimism

People tend to forecast what they hope will happen as well as what they think will happen.

A seminal study showing this was by Hayes in 1936[45]. He showed that two weeks before the 1932 Presidential election, 84% of factory workers who intended to vote for Hoover thought he would win. Meanwhile only 6% of those not intending to vote for Hoover thought he would win.

§

In 1970, J. B. Kidd[46] found that engineers were optimistic in forecasting the time it would take to overhaul electric generators. The estimated time was generally 60% of the actual time required. This despite the fact that the estimates were made after the projects were well under way.

§

In 1934, William Ogburn[47] found that students of losing football teams had forecasted their teams would lose by an average of 3 points. The average defeats averaged 18 points. Students at the winning colleges had forecasted victories by an average of 6 points.

§

In 1955, Thor Hultgren[48] examined quarterly forecasts of freight shipped over railways from 1927 to 1952. The forecasters were 'experts' employed by the railway companies. Forecasts were heavily biased towards good business ranging from 41% too high to 2% too low.

Judges pay too much attention to trends

As well as being optimistic, judgements fail to be conservative on trends. Judges tend to overestimate the degree to which today's trends will persist into the future.

A study by Franco Modigliani and Owen Sauerlender in 1955[49] (who examined the same railway forecasts mentioned above) showed how optimism and conservatism can combine. They found that when shipments were rising, forecasts underestimated by 5%. However, when shipments were falling they overestimated by 16%. On average, the estimates were 4% too high.

The problem of 'availability' with judges

Human brains have a problem in that the thing they are currently thinking about tends to be accorded undue significance. This is known as the 'availability error'.

For example, consider this simple but elegant little experiment[50]t. One group of subjects was asked to estimate quickly:

$$8 \times 7 \times 6 \times 4 \times 3 \times 2 \times 1$$

On average they estimated the answer to be 2250. Then a second group was asked to estimate:

$$1 \times 2 \times 3 \times 4 \times 5 \times 6 \times 7 \times 8$$

On average they estimated just 512

The reason is that the groups focussed on the numbers at the beginning of the calculation. When the numbers at the beginning are big, they are accorded undue weight and the answer is too big. When the numbers at the beginning are small, they are accorded undue weight and the answer is too big.

So, if people focus on forecasting the sales of one product, they will accord it undue significance and tend to over-estimate its sales. Unfortunately, this is exactly what people do do when they are making judgement forecasts for their products. (Recall my earlier example of the asthma market where individual companies' sales forecasts added up to nearly 200% of the market.) This is consistent with a general principle. Judges do not normalise their responses (i.e. they do not take into account all the other judgements they could make and ensure consistency).

If you ask people to give you the probability of a number of mutually exclusive and totally exhaustive events, the probabilities should add up to 100%. But, they tend to add up to much more. In yet another study[51] where ten choices were given, the total probability was 288%.

Principle 3: Keep it Simple

The Nobel Laureate, Herbert Simon said that 'The capacity of the human mind for formulating and solving complex problems is very small compared with the size of problems whose solution is required...in the real world.' Even the greatest expert has only a limited perception of all the things that will affect an uncertain future. And yet a lot of money is spent on advisory panels and syndicated expert reports. Leading experts are used to forecast the way ahead. There is no evidence that this produces better forecasts.

Scott Armstrong[5] has reviewed the relationship between expertise and accuracy in forecasting change: 'Many studies have been done on the value of experts. Most have come from psychology and finance, but there is evidence also from economics, medicine, sports and other areas. Expertise in the field of interest has been measured in various ways (education, experience, reputation, previous success, self-identification). Accuracy has also been measured in many ways. With few exceptions, the results fall into the [same] pattern...Above a low level of expertise...(which can be obtained quickly and easily), expertise and accuracy are almost unrelated...Of course, expertise does add to the comfort level of the client. A positive relationship would be expected between the client's confidence and the money spent on experts.'

§

One marketing example from more than a hundred studies that pretty well all support the above summary: A 1977 study found that two students and a housewife were as accurate predicting which mail survey items would be subject to non-response bias as were nine faculty members who had substantial experience with survey research[52].

Research into how much information judges need to make the most accurate predictions parallels that on the level of expertise. Beyond a minimal amount of information, additional information does not add to accuracy. It does, however, add to cost. Much of the evidence comes from psychology, but evidence is also available from the field of marketing.

For example, a 1970's study tested two survey types to investigate people's intention to subscribe to a new sort of public transport called the Minicar system. (Rather than own a car, you just picked one up a small fuel-efficient car from a nearby garage and drove it to the garage closest to your destination.) The simple survey involved mailing a 'brief' description of the service with a picture of the car. The comprehensive survey required the subject to attend a product clinic. They were shown graphs, sat in the vehicle, watched a movie and were allowed to question guides. The comprehensive survey cost about ten times the simple survey. But there was no difference between intentions to purchase.

Principle 4: Look at the Problem from Many Angles

It makes sense to use a number of judges (with a variety of perspectives). The evidence suggests that this is the best approach.

- The literature, on balance, suggests that five to ten experts is the optimal number[53].
- Empirical studies have suggested between five and nine[54].
- Theoretical arguments have been used to suggest no less than six and no more than twenty experts should be used.
- You should theoretically tend towards the higher end of the range if your experts differ among one another in their forecasts and if they can make good forecasts.
- A good rule of thumb is to use ten experts[55],.

The principle of combining these different judgements applies just as strongly as for other forms of forecasting.

Scott Armstrong has concluded that: 'The evidence on the value of combining is impressive, and it comes from a variety of areas. As long as the judges possess a minimum level of expertise, combining is better than the average accuracy of the component forecasts.'[5]

But note that we are talking here about combining forecasts from a number of judges with different perspectives. Getting half a dozen sales forecasts from different members of the marketing department won't help!

Principle 5: Use Scientific Tools Scientifically

Sometimes, judges are asked to give estimates of the uncertainty of their forecasts. These numerical probability ratings give a veneer of scientific respectability to their guesses.

We have already looked at this problem to an extent and at the way that Monte Carlo simulations using experts' judgements of uncertainty are spurious. To repeat: *__experts are no good at estimating the uncertainty of their forecasts.__*

As far back as 1950, Kaplan, Skogstat and Girshick[56] found a rank correlation of only 0.2 between a measure of confidence provided by each judge and their accuracy in forecasting social and technological events.

§

In 1972, Stael von Holstein[57] asked experts to forecast changes in share prices and to give 99% confidence limits. 43% of the actual changes fell outside the 99% confidence limits. Feedback was then provided so that the judges could see that their confidence limits were much too narrow. They did get a bit better, but still 23% of changes fell outside their 99% confidence limits.

Sometimes agreement amongst judges is used as a proxy for the uncertainty in a forecast. This can be very dangerous, particularly if the judges share the same backgrounds (and therefore prejudices) and are allowed to interact and therefore 'flock' together.

As an example, here is an account of how designers at Ford forecast the public's response to a new car design:
'The final concept as it looked in plaster was satisfying to every designer in the company, and when you get 800 stylists under one roof to agree that they like a creation, you have unusually high agreement,'[58]
The car was launched as the Edsel and is famous as one of the biggest ever marketing disasters.

Principle 6: Use Techniques Proven to Work in the Real World

Although informal (judgement) forecasts are generally not very good, there are ways to make them less bad. These techniques are useful because sometimes – when there is little objective data – you have little choice but to make informal forecasts.

Under these circumstances, you might use managers, customers or 'experts' to provide your judgements. What ever you choose, the same principles apply.

Avoiding biased judges

Don't use experts who have a vested interest in the outcome of the forecast. (We have already seen – and will see in what follows – that people can be unduly optimistic when they have a vested interest.)

And you can very easily bias the judges yourself by posing questions in a leading fashion. Many subtle ways of inadvertently introducing bias into a question exist. Anything that smacks of a value judgement on the part of the questioner will tend to elicit answers that confirm it.

For example, in one study[59], people were shown a basket ball player and asked his height in one of two ways. Some were asked, 'How tall was the basket ball player?' and answered on average 79 inches. Others were asked, 'How short was the basket ball player?' and answered on average 69 inches.

Don't ask questions which give the judge the opportunity to try to 'look good'

Part of the folk lore of market research is that the major pollutant is people trying to please the researcher. Maybe this flatters the ego of market researchers. The evidence points in another direction. The key pollutant when you are trying to get honest judgements from people (particularly intentions) is people trying to look good.

Elliot Aronson and Thomas Van Hoose performed a sham experiment in 1970 to determine whether co-operating or looking good are more important to subjects[60].

They got students to see how fast they could copy out lists of telephone numbers. The students tried hard and performed better than in an initial practice session both in enhanced lighting conditions (which – it was 'leaked' was supposed to increase performance) and reduced lighting conditions (which was supposed to decrease performance.)

The opportunity to 'please' the researchers by confirming the results they were looking for, did not seem to affect performance. Then, when 'leaked' the fact that the experiment was trying to confirm that obsessive, compulsive people are better at mindless tasks like copying out telephone numbers, the subjects suddenly stopped trying to do well and their performance plummeted.

People don't know how they would act in an unfamiliar situation – so don't ask them

A central problem with market research is that it relies on asking people to say what they would do in the real world. What people say they would do and what they actually do are quite different things. We have already seen that – for example – answers are polluted by respondents trying to look good. Things get far worse when you ask them about unfamiliar situations. The problem then is that they don't know themselves what they would do.

In 1966, Charles Hofling and co-workers[61] asked 33 nurses what they would do if an unfamiliar doctor telephoned them and told them to give a patient a medicine that was not on the hospital formulary and at twice the maximum recommended dose shown on the pack. All but two of the nurses said that they would not give the medicine. However, when a field experiment was performed on 22 comparable nurses, only one of them refused to administer the drug.

This study was replicated by Steven Rank and Cardell Jacobson in 1977[62]. This time it was made easier for the nurses to disobey: they were familiar with the drug and they could get peer group support from their colleagues not to obey. And yet still, if the doctor insisted, half the nurses were prepared to follow orders.

The logical conclusion must be that in unclear situations, it is best not to ask people for their intentions. It turns out that it is probably better to ask them for their opinions on what will happen generally rather than what they as individuals intend to do. Intentions are favoured when:

- The decision is important. (Intentions are much better at predicting sales of cars than of butter.)
- The respondent has a plan. (Engagements are a good predictor of marriage, capital expenditure budgets for X-ray machines are a good predictor of sales.)

- The respondent is likely to answer forthrightly. (In a classic 1934 study[63] R. T. LaPiere and a Chinese couple visited 250 hotels and restaurants. They were refused service once. He then sent a questionnaire to the same establishments asking whether Chinese customers were welcome. 92% of the respondents said 'no'.)
- The respondent has the power to fulfil his intention. Junior doctors might intend to use our drug, but the hospital formulary committee might not let them.
- Circumstances are not likely to change. (There is absolutely no point asking doctors whether they intend to use a product that is currently in phase II development when the competitive backdrop by the time it is launched is likely to be radically different.)

This all implies that intentions are useful in certain circumstances and in the short term. (Circumstances will almost always change in the long term). It is also a prerequisite that 'intenders' should be easily identified.

When intentions are not appropriate, the more useful form of judgement is an opinion.

Scenarios have no magical powers in forecasting

Scenario planning is very much in vogue. It has been popularised particularly by Peter Schwarz who wrote *The Art of the Long View*[64] (a book based on the approach to long term planning practised by the oil giant Shell). Whilst there is evidence to show that scenarios open people's minds to the possibilities of an outcome occurring (we noted this earlier.), there seems to be no evidence for or against scenario writing as a means to provide accurate forecasts[5].

However, the more scenarios you map out the greater the chance that one of them will be right! Indeed Schwarz himself failed to recognise this benefit when in the summer of 1997 he abandoned the scenario planners usual caution and forecast a 25 year "long boom"[65]. Just one year later Asian economies were contracting, Russia's economy was in free-fall and world stock markets' long bull run was faltering.

The least popular and least costly survey methods may give you the best results in forecasting

Market research companies have a strong bias towards large face to face surveys. This is presumably because they make a lot of money on them. The evidence, however, suggests that this is often not the best route to employ.

Generally, research suggests that for most issues, responses from mail, telephone and personal interviews are similar[5].

However, where sensitive issues - including issues where 'looking good' is involved, mail is generally superior.

Indeed Seymore Sudman and Norman Bradborn[66] conducted a huge statistical analysis of 935 published studies and concluded that for threatening questions, it is best to use self administered questionnaires that are completed with no one else present and preferably not at work or anywhere where there is a line of authority.

§

A poignant example of how mail questionnaires can elicit franker responses comes from Frederick Wiseman[67] who reported that 75% of Catholics were in favour of birth control when surveyed by mail as compared to only 44% when interviewed by either phone or in person.

Structured groups may be useful in poorly defined situations

Groups are difficult things to get right. Groups are a social event. They may provide a caricatured version of the real world. And they are prone to be dominated by a few individuals. Conventional wisdom has it that groups are better at coming up with creative ideas. There is, however, evidence to call this into question. Also, there is the very real danger that the group can float free from reality as the members vie to impress each other.

Groups of people are more concerned with power and conformity than they are with the task in hand.

In 1932, Arthur Jenness[68] got people to estimate the number of beans in a jar individually and in groups. The groups agreed with each other, but produced less accurate forecasts. This result has often been confirmed: traditional group meetings improve agreement, but not accuracy.

Unstructured group meetings, in particular, can do more harm than good.

Norman Dalkey[69] compared the accuracy of individual 'backcasts' (using current data to try to 'forecast' what the situation was in the past) to those obtained from a group. He used data from almanacs. He found that the individual backcasts were more accurate than the group forecasts.

But structuring meetings in a pseudo-scientific way does not help. The Delphi method is a case in point.

The Delphi method is named after the ancient Greek oracle. It was invented in 1948 by researchers at the Rand Corporation. It involves obtaining forecasts from a number of judges, and then letting the judges see each other's forecasts and reasoning. New forecasts are then obtained and the process is repeated until a consensus is achieved. The technique sounds reasonable and its name and pedigree give it a veneer of reliability. However, in an extensive review of past studies into the Delphi technique, Fred Woudenberg[70], an experimental psychologist, concluded that 'no evidence was found that Delphi is more accurate than other judgement methods'.

The problem with Delphi forecasts seems to be the same as the problem with groups in general: groups are social events and dominance and conformity become more important than the task in hand. In experiments with Delphi forecasting where the answers to the problem were known, the consensus converged on the initial group median rather than on the correct answer[71].

If groups are to work well, there are a number of guidelines that do seem to help. There is no exact magic formula or structure, but these common elements seem to work well:

1. 'Establish openness and participation
2. Encourage many and diverse ideas
3. Build on each other's ideas
4. Orientate towards problems
5. Use a leader to guide discussion'[72]

Role playing can be very helpful especially in situations where interaction is important

We have now seen that problems – like people wanting to 'look good' and not knowing how they will act in uncertain situations – hamper judgement forecasts. It turns out that there is a technique which – the evidence suggests – tends to work much better than surveys or groups. That technique is role-playing.

The idea of role-playing might sound silly. Particularly when you face a serious situation. There is no graver situation than war. And yet, during the Vietnam conflict, high ranking US military officers chose to play a role play game[73]. They split into two groups: one represented the US, the other North Vietnam. The role-play suggested that limited bombing of the North Vietnamese was the poorest strategy and worse than no bombing at all. The decision-makers chose to ignore the game and opted for limited bombing. It was a disaster.

Although it seems frivolous, the record for role play as a means to produce forecasts - particularly where there is interaction between people and groups - is very good.

One review [5], compared the accuracy of opinion and role play derived prediction in seven different circumstances: out of 121 opinion based predictions, 20% were correct; out of 189 role-playing predictions, 70% were correct.

One example relates to pharmaceuticals.

In a 1977 study[74], subjects were asked to try to predict the actions of the board of the Upjohn Corporation. Upjohn marketed a product called Panalba. New data suggested strongly that the drug had harmful side effects. Subjects had to decide on one of five courses of action:
1. Recall Panalba
2. Stop production, but allow existing stocks to be sold.
3. Stop all advertising and promotion, but continue to supply the drug.
4. Continue to market the drug actively until it is banned.
5. Continue to market the drug actively and lobby and take legal action to prevent the authorities banning the drug.

Of 57 groups that role played the board's deliberations, none removed the drug from the market and 79% took decision 5. In fact, Upjohn did take decision 5, but the Supreme Court later forced them to take Panalba off the market.

Of 71 respondents to an interview - who had not role played the situation - only 2% said they would select decision 5 and more than half said they would choose decision 1.

Of 46 respondents to an opinion survey, 41% predicted that Upjohn would take option 5.

Most of the favourable studies into role-playing have asked people to act as *they* would act in that role (rather than asking them to act as they think that someone else would act). So, it appears that the role – rather than trying to 'look good' – dominates their behaviour[5].

Summary of valid approaches to informal (subjective) forecasting

We conclude this review of informal forecasting with a summary of which approach might be best for your circumstances.

When the problem is clear and judges are not self-conscious over the issue, then the traditional survey will suffice. However, if the judges are self-conscious (in particular they are likely to try to 'look good'), if the problem is poorly defined or if the situation involves uncertainty and interactions amongst the players, then the different approaches covered here could be rated roughly as follows:

RATING OF JUDGEMENT FORECAST TECHNIQUES ACCORDING TO SITUATION (THE MORE STARS THE BETTER)

	Judges self conscious	Poorly defined problem	Situation involves uncertainty and interaction
Personal interview	*	**	*
Impersonal interview (telephone or mail)	**	*	*
Group discussion	*	***	**
Role play	***	**	***

Chapter 3

Chapter 3: Extrapolation models: how history can be your guide to the future in stable situations

A trend is a trend is a trend
But the question is, will it bend?
Will it alter its course
Through some unforeseen force
And come to a premature end?
Cairncross (1969)

This chapter seeks to answer just this question.

Extrapolation Models vs. Causal Models

If you have decided you want to use a model rather than an informal forecast (you have got some data and there is some degree of change ahead) you need to decide whether to use an extrapolation model or a causal model.

An extrapolation model projects historical patterns into the future. A causal method assumes that the thing you are trying to predict is *caused* by something and estimates the relationship between the thing you are trying to forecast and the things that cause it to vary. (Obviously, causal models will be of particular interest to you if you want to affect the future through – for example – your marketing or development programs.)

Experts like to build causal – particularly 'econometric' – models. (We will cover what econometric models are later.) So, if you ask forecasting experts whether econometric models are better than extrapolation models, the results are not surprising. (This is a great example of why you shouldn't use biased judges!). The results of what 21 experts thought in a survey[5] are shown in the following table:

EXPERTS VIEWS OF WHICH TYPE OF MODEL IS BEST

Econometric forecasts rated as…	Proportion of experts agreeing
Significantly more accurate	33%
Somewhat more accurate	62%
No difference	0%
Somewhat less accurate	5%
Significantly less accurate	0%

But although these judges are clearly biased, in this instance their views are broadly correct.

Empirical evidence suggests that on balance, causal models are better at forecasting than extrapolation models. However, their superiority really emerges when there are big changes and in the long term. In the short term there is little to choose between the two types of model. There follow the results from a survey[5] of studies that compared extrapolation and causal models. (The results shown here include only the studies that were judged to constitute an adequate test.)

STUDIES COMPARING EXTRAPOLATION AND CAUSAL MODELS

	Extrapolation models better	No difference	Causal models better
Small environmental change	16	11	13
Large environmental change	0	1	8

The results make perfect intuitive sense. When there is little change, it is relatively easy to forecast and there is little difference between methods. If anything, just extrapolating the current trend might be preferable. (It is certainly easier.) However, when things are changing, extrapolating a trend is not a good way to forecast.

How odd then that many of the syndicated forecasts for pharmaceutical markets are extrapolation forecasts with judgement superimposed on them – a combination of the two least useful forms of forecasting for the long term!

There are two other issues that you need to consider in choosing between an extrapolation and a causal model. First, you have to be realistic about the data you have. If you can only get your hands on past data for the dependent variable (the thing you are trying to predict – for example patient numbers) you are forced in the direction of an extrapolation forecast. Second, if what you want to know is how you can alter the situation or the trend by your own marketing efforts, you are forced in the direction of a causal forecast.

If, in the light of all this, you have a situation that favours extrapolation (little environmental change and good data restricted to the variable you want to forecast), you will once again make better forecasts if you follow the six principles of good forecasting:

How the "six principles" apply to extrapolation forecasts

Principle 1: Break the Problem Down

Often extrapolation requires us to break down past sales into separate components in order to effectively extrapolate into the future. For example, sales patterns are often the result of a long-term trend and seasonal fluctuations around that trend. The best approach to extrapolating here is to decompose sales into the trend and the seasonal factors. You can then extrapolate the long-term trend and then add back the seasonal factors.

For example, consider a hay fever product that is growing long term, but sells far more in summer than winter. We can calculate the sales for the average of all months. Then, we can calculate the average sales for every January, every February, every March and so on. We can then calculate a "seasonal factor" for each month by dividing the average sales for that month by the average for all months. So, if July has a seasonal factor of 140%, this means that sales in July are 40% higher than sales in the average month.

Now, if we every monthly sales value by the seasonal factor for the month in question, we will generate a deseasonalized trend. We can then extrapolate this trend. We then simply add back seasonality by multiplying each monthly forecast by the appropriate monthly seasonal factor.

The following figure shows this idea pictorially.

A SEASONAL PHARMACEUTICAL'S SALES PATTERN

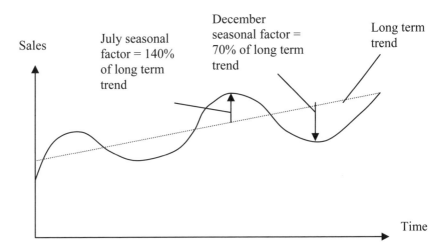

Principle 2: Be Conservative

Extrapolation models use past data to compute a trend and then use that trend to project into the future. The principle of conservatism suggests to us that you should be suspicious of such a trend (as it is taking us further and further away from the current situation and things tend not to change as much as we think they will).

Empirical evidence suggests that this is true.

> Empirical evidence that damping trends improves the accuracy of extrapolation forecasts emerged in the 1980s. Two early workers, Everette Gardner and Ed. McKenzie noted that, 'recent empirical findings suggest that accuracy can be improved by either damping or ignoring altogether trends which have a low probability of persistence'. They went on to test a version of exponential smoothing which damped the trend and found that it outperformed all the other more sophisticated models it was compared with[75].

Principle 3: Keep it Simple

Stephen Schnaars of the City University of New York has reviewed the relative performance of different types of extrapolation models, and concluded that: 'The overwhelming conclusion of these comparisons has been that there is no advantage to methodological complexity … Simple models appear to provide forecasts that are at least as accurate as more complex approaches.'[76]

Schnaar's conclusion is supported by a review of all the studies that compared extrapolation techniques between 1960 and 1985[5]. It showed the following:

STUDIES COMPARING COMPLEX AND SIMPLE EXTRAPOLATION MODELS

Study outcome	Number of studies
Complex methods (Box-Jenkins, adaptive parameters etc.) better	8
No difference	17
Simple methods (MAT, exponential smoothing, constant parameters etc.) better	9

The author of this survey, Scott Armstrong, concluded in a later paper that: 'there has been a negligible gain in accuracy from the use of sophisticated methods...time and money would have been saved had highly sophisticated methods been avoided'[33].

Indeed, it has even been shown that the cheapest and simplest extrapolation method you can conceive of – 'eyeballing' – is up there with the best.

'Subjective extrapolation' is forecasting jargon for 'eyeballing' (looking at a past trend and just guestimating the future trend. Generally, there appears to be little to choose between 'eyeballing' and more complex extrapolation methods – some studies favour the one and others the other[5]. The biggest and most useful study [77] compared eyeballing with extrapolations in 111 of the time series from the famous M-competition. (You will learn more about this later.) In general 'eyeballing' was at least as good as formal methods. But formal methods tend to win through in long term forecasts. (Interestingly, subjects provided slightly more accurate forecasts when presented with tables rather than graphs.)

Principle 4: Look at the Problem from Many Angles

Stephen Schnaars says about extrapolation forecasts that: 'One of the most consistent findings of comparative studies has been that combinations of forecasts are more accurate than individual models...In addition, most studies have found that a simple average of models is superior to a combination that tries to weight the individual models that are used to construct it. This suggests that the philosophy of 'eclectic' research has merit, but that implementing it with anything more than the most rudimentary schemes does not pay off.'

Once again, there is a large body of evidence backing up this assertion

Schnaars himself went on to add further evidence by investigating the accuracy of a basket of forecasting models on 103 data series. He confirmed the above principle and also showed that for mature products and durable products the model that best predicts future sales is the pompously titled 'random walk model' which merely assumes that future sales will be exactly the same as the latest available sales figure.

§

Scott Armstrong[78] has reviewed evidence from a quarter of a century of extrapolation forecasting experience. He compared the accuracy of extrapolation forecasts alone and in combination and found an average error reduction of 42% when two methods were combined.

§

In 1983, Spyros Makridakis and Robert Winkler[79] published their findings on how combining extrapolation forecasts improved accuracy. They used 111 time series from their famous M-competition. (Again, more on this later.) They found that the average forecast error was reduced by 7.2% when two methods were combined, with continuing (but diminishing) gains as more and more methods were added. For example, a 16.3% reduction was seen with five methods.

Furthermore, the more dissimilar the forecast methods, the greater the gains to be had by combining them. And because the forecasts produced by different methods diverge more and more over time, it is not surprising that combining extrapolation forecasts is most helpful over the long term[5].

Principle 5: Use Scientific Tools Scientifically

The key point to stress here is that the errors using past data are not the same as the errors to be expected in the future.

The uncertainty in extrapolation forecasts is often estimated by seeing how closely an extrapolation model fits past data. We have to be very cautious about using such an unscientific device. Such estimates of uncertainty do tend to be reasonably accurate[80] but *only in the short term and providing there are no changes in the environment*[5]. This makes good intuitive sense.

Principle 6: Use Techniques Proven to Work in the Real World

There are many off-the-shelf computer packages that will examine past data, find the mathematical curve that best fits the past data and extrapolate it into the future. This is not your objective. You want the models that best fit future data. There are no guarantees, but surely your best bet is to go with the techniques that have worked best in proper studies.

Before, we look at specific models however, we have to clean and process the data…

Cleaning and processing data for extrapolation models

The key task in cleaning the data is to look for outliers – data that are worryingly high or low. The key task in processing the data is to adjust for seasonality. We now review how to handle these issues simply and practically.

Outliers

If you find any outliers, you ought to take the following steps

1. Look to see if there is a simple error (keypunch error is often the cause).
2. Look for corroborating data (look in an annual report for sales figures as well as an audit).
3. Look for inconsistencies that could cause abrupt jumps and inconsistencies. For example, German data may be for Western Germany for early data points and for the united Germany for later data points.
4. If you are still unsure about the data, consider tempering the effect of the outlier. There are many methods. One simple method that you can use is 'windsorizing'. Here you simply make the outliers no more extreme than the most extreme data that you believe is accurately measured.

Seasonality

Many products display seasonality. For example, hay fever products sell more in the summer. The way to forecast seasonality is to determine the seasonal factor for each time period (month or quarter for example). The seasonal factor for a month is how much bigger sales are in that month compared to the average for the year. So, if average monthly sales are 20,000 units per month and the (multiplicative) seasonal factors for July and December are 2 and 0.3 respectively, then forecast sales for July are 20,000 x 2 = 40,000 and for December are 20,000 x 0.3 = 6,000.

Seasonal factors can be created in many ways. A simple solution is to apply regression analysis where the months are represented as 'dummy variables', and their relationship to, say, the moving annual total calculated. The seasonal factors can be stated as either multiplicative (e.g. July sales tend to be 150% of the MAT) or additive (e.g. July sales tend to be 60,000 packs higher than the MAT). Multiplicative factors tend to be favoured by economists. (But, if you have big errors or if there is not a very strong trend you might be better with additive factors.)

The major difference between extrapolation models

We now move onto specific extrapolation models. We will concentrate on the simple, effective models that the forecasting literature suggests will give you the best results. The major difference between the key models is the weights they give to past data. The following cartoon summarises the way that four simple models apply different weights to past data. In the cartoon we have nine years of past data (Y-1 being last year and Y-9 being nine years ago). The size of the blob in each year indicates the relative weight that each extrapolation method would give to data from that year.

A SUMMARY OF EXTRAPOLATION TECHNIQUES

	Y-7	Y-6	Y-5	Y-4	Y-3	Y-2	Y-1
Random walk							●
Exponential smoothing	·	·	●	●	●	●	●
Moving average (4 year here)				●	●	●	●
Regression	●	●	●	●	●	●	●

As you can see, the Random Walk Model places all the weighting on the last data point; exponential smoothing places weight on all data points, but the weighting falls off as you go back in time; moving averages place an equal amount of weight on a specified number of recent data points; and regression analysis places equal weightings on all past data points.

The weightings used by exponential smoothing are to many people intuitively the most satisfactory. And – as you will see – such intuition is well placed.

Random Walk Model

The Random Walk Model is the simplest extrapolation model imaginable. It simply forecasts that the sales in the next period (and all subsequent periods) will be equal to the sales in the last period. This makes sense when there is no trend and movements from the current position are purely random. Given that it is as likely that sales will go up as down, the best forecast, on average, will be the current sales level.

In many mature markets the total market volume *does* follow a random walk[81] and this simplest of models is useful.

Usually, however, there is a trend and that is where the other models come in.

Exponential Smoothing Model

If you have to choose a single method for extrapolation, you would be best advised to use exponential smoothing. Unfortunately textbooks usually do not explain how to use this technique properly. Therefore some space is dedicated here to a simple description of exponential smoothing. (The EviCast forecasting package for pharmaceuticals contains a user-friendly version of exponential smoothing.)

How to do exponential smoothing

Exponential smoothing is similar to a moving average (with which you are almost certainly familiar). But, it places more weight on the most recent data. The weighting on each previous period drops off exponentially (typically by about 25% for each preceding period). So the older the data, the less influence it has on the forecast. Such a weighting appeals to common sense and is supported by empirical studies[82].

The details of how to perform exponential smoothing are now outlined. Even though the concept is simple, the detail can be quite heavy going. You are advised to read this only if you want to construct an Exponential Smoothing Model *now*. Otherwise, just make a mental note that you know where to look when you need to.

> The smoothed average is calculated using three pieces of data: the current actual, the smoothed average for the last period and a so-called 'smoothing constant'. The new smoothed average is given by:
> (the current actual x smoothing constant) + (the preceding smoothed average) x (1 – smoothing constant)
> Let us say that the smoothing constant is 0.25 (generally figures between 0.2 and 0.3 give the best results. Without going into the arithmetic, this is what results: our new 'smoothed average' is a weighted average of all the past actuals. The current actual provides 25% of the weight, the preceding actual 25% less than this (about 19%), the

preceding actual 25% less than this (about 14%) and so forth. You can see that the weight accorded to each actual is dropping off by a constant proportion (25% in this case) i.e. exponentially. Hence 'exponential smoothing'.

In a situation where there is no trend upwards or downwards this smoothed average is used as the forecast. (Most textbooks teach exponential forecasting this way.) But if there is a trend, then an exponentially smoothed trend is calculated in just the same way as the smoothed average. The actual trend for a given period is the increase or decrease in the smoothed average since the preceding period. The smoothed trend is calculated in the same way as the smoothed average:

(the current actual) x (smoothing constant) + (preceding smoothed average) x (1 – smoothing constant).

In practice there seems to be little to gain from having different smoothing factors for the average and the trend.

Future forecasts are then produced by taking the last smoothed average and extrapolating out using the last smoothed trend. (If an additive trend is used, the trend is added to the last smooth average; if a geometric trend is used, the last smoothed average is multiplied by (1 + trend)).

However, things are not quite this simple. If there is a trend, the smoothed average tends to lag behind the actuals. So, an adjustment needs to be made. Robert Brown suggested an adjustment that has stood the test of time back in 1959[83, 84]. The current smoothed average is increased by the current smoothed trend multiplied by (1 – smoothing constant)/smoothing constant.

Some practical pointers on exponential smoothing

We now cover some practical pointers for constructing effective exponential smoothing models. Again, I would recommend that you don't go into the detail now unless you are actually constructing a model now.

Firstly, accuracy can – as we have seen – be improved by damping the trend according to our uncertainty in it.

So, you might multiply the trend by 1 if you are totally certain that it will persist, by 0 if you have no confidence in it and by 0.5 if you are vaguely uneasy about it. You should be especially suspicious of trends, and therefore damp them more, in long term forecasts.

Secondly, there are useful rules of thumb on how to choose a smoothing constant.

Generally, the smoothing factor is between 0.2 and 0.3. It can be selected using historical data to determine which constant gives the 'best fit'. However, there is no empirical evidence to suggest that this leads to better forecasts[5].

Generally, the smoothing factor should be selected as follows;

HOW TO SELECT THE SMOOTHING CONSTANT FOR EXPONENTIAL SMOOTHING

	High smoothing constant	Low smoothing constant
Historical pattern	Unstable	Stable
Measurement error	Low	High
Time periods	Long	Short

Thirdly, there are rules of thumb as to how much past data you need to make meaningful forecasts.

There are two such rules of thumb: Ayre's rule says that if you want to forecast n periods ahead, you need n periods of historical data. Armstrong's rule suggests that you need relatively more data for short-term forecasts. So, the number of historical data points that you need to forecast n periods ahead is $4\sqrt{n}$.

Empirical studies looking at business, financial and economic forecasts all suggest that Armstrong's rule is a better pointer to the optimum number of data points required[82, 85-88].

If there is a lot of historical data (more than (2 – smoothing constant)/(smoothing constant) observations, the starting value decision is not very important. If there is less historic data than this, your guestimate of a starting value could be material and you should do some sensitivity modelling.

Lastly, there are rules of thumb as to whether you should use an additive or a multiplicative (geometrical or exponential) trend

The following is a useful guide in the short term.

WHETHER TO USE AN ADDITIVE OR EXPONENTIAL TREND

	Additive	Exponential
Data value	Any	All > 0
Data type	Interval or ratio	Ratio
Measurement error	Large	Small
A priori growth assumption	Linear	Geometric

Moving Average Model

We now move on to an even simpler – and more familiar model – than exponential smoothing. Moving averages are similar to exponential smoothing. But each data point is weighted equally and back data is only considered for a given period. For example, a three year moving average considers the last three years of data, a four year moving average considers the last four years of data.

The advantages of moving averages is that they are easier to understand and seasonality can be removed by using an average that incorporates a whole number of complete cycles: typically one or more years.

The disadvantage is that empirical studies have suggested that they are less accurate than exponential smoothing.

This empirical data includes the famous 'M-competition'. In 1982 Spyros Makridakis and co-workers published the results of a huge comparative study of extrapolation methods[89]. They compared 21 different methods against 1001 different time series. Although simple methods fared well, moving averages were not particularly impressive.

Regression Model

Another popular extrapolation method is regression analysis. Here a regression analysis (which fits a line so as to minimise the variance of data points from the line) is run using time as the independent variable.

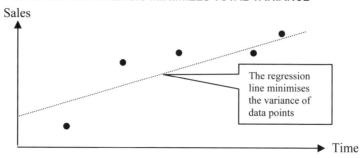

REGRESSION ANALYSIS MINIMIZES TOTAL VARIANCE

The problem with regression is that it gives equal weight to all data points. Perhaps as a result, empirical data has shown that the forecasting accuracy of regressions against time is slightly inferior to that of exponential smoothing[5].

Box Jenkins Model

A brief word about one very complicated extrapolation model is in order. Box-Jenkins is – according to the few that understand it – theoretically the gold standard in extrapolation methods. It works a bit like the control methods in chemical processing plants. The difference between the actual state and the desired state is analysed and adjustments are made based on the difference. In the case of Box-Jenkins the analysis is between the most recent observation and recent forecasts.

However, empirical evidence suggests that it does not outperform simpler more intuitive models[5].

Markov Chain Model

Another complicated approach to extrapolation is Markov chains. (You may have encountered these in the context of health economics, but they are also used in forecasting.) Markov chains take current patterns of behaviour and extrapolate them into the future. To do this, they see people as being in one of a number of states. In each period of time, they have a given probability of either staying in that state or of moving to one of the other states. Importantly, the system is deemed to have no memory of past states. For each cycle, a subject in a given state has exactly the same probability of staying in that state or moving to other states, irrespective of the states he or she has occupied in previous cycles. This is rather unrealistic and may explain why Markov chains have such a poor record in forecasting.

In our circumstances this implies that a doctor's awareness, trial and usage patterns are not affected by past history. Evidence from the marketing literature strongly suggests that this is wrong[90].

- The earlier a buyer becomes aware, the more likely he is to try the product.
- The earlier a buyer tries a product, the more likely he/she is to be a long-term repeat purchaser.
- The earlier a buyer adopts a product, the more likely he/she will be a heavy user.
- The more often a buyer has repeat purchased, the more likely he/she is to repeat purchase in the future.

A technical explanation of Markov chains requires matrix mathematics and so is not covered here. If you want to use 'flow' models, you so not need a technical understanding as there is very simple software that will do it for you. A good package tailored to pharmaceutical forecasting is Inpharmation's EviCast

Markov chains can be difficult to understand and require heroic assumptions. More importantly, there is very little empirical evidence to support their value in anything other than the short term. One review concluded that 'This technique and similar ones have been recommended frequently for predictions in marketing when people are assumed to go through various states in using a product (e.g., trial, repeat purchase and adoption). Unfortunately, despite many publications on Markov and related models, little research on their predictive value was found.'[5]

Ranking of extrapolation methods

To summarise the foregoing evidence, we can rank the various extrapolation techniques as follows:

RANKING OF EXTRAPOLATION TECHNIQUES

Method	Easy to understand	Accuracy of forecast short term	Accuracy of forecast long term
Exponential smoothing	OK	1=	1
Moving average	Easy	3=	3
Box-Jenkins	Difficult	1=	2
Regressions	OK	3=	4
Markov chains	Quite difficult	5	5

In the light of all this, it seems sensible to equip ourselves with a really good exponential smoothing module.

Putting it into practice

There are many good software packages that allow you to extrapolate quickly and easily. EviCast, from my own company Inpharmation, is perhaps the simplest and is designed specifically for pharma forecasters.

EVICAST IS PERHAPS THE EASIEST SOLUTION FOR PHARMA EXTRAPOLATION

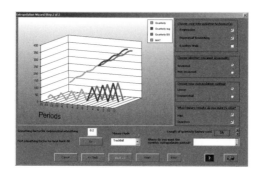

Chapter 4: Segmentation models – the big disappointment in forecasting

There never were, in the world, two opinions alike.
No more than two hairs, or two grains;
The most universal quality is diversity.
Jean Giraudoux

If you have decided not to use informal methods (you have some data and can build a model) and not to build an extrapolation model (you expect – or want to bring about change) you are going to want to build a causal model.

Your first decision is whether to use the differences between different parts of the market as your causes (to build a segmentation model) or whether to consider causes that apply in aggregate across the whole market (an aggregate model).

We begin with a comparison of these two approaches. The results are counterintuitive to experienced marketers. We are taught that segmenting a market is one of the most important jobs of marketing (if not *the* most important jobs in marketing). We might also expect that it is one of the best ways to forecast. Prepare to be surprised by the evidence.

Segmentation models vs. "aggregate" models

An aggregate model proposes that the thing you are trying to forecast is *caused* by forces that apply and are measured across the whole market or population that you are dealing with. It may, at its simplest, take a form such as: 'If advertising goes up 1%, sales will go up 0.2%' (this incidentally is often a very useful forecasting model).

A segmentation model, on the other hand, assumes that the thing you are trying to forecast is *caused* by differences between different parts of the market or population you are dealing with. For example, gastroenterologists will put all their patients on this drug, GPs will put none of their patients on this drug.

The clear conclusion from the forecasting literature is that aggregate models make better use of the available data. There are many more studies attesting to successful aggregate models than to successful segmentation models. Because segmentation models have proven surprisingly disappointing, there are few comparative studies between aggregate models and segmentation models. A review or the few studies in the forecasting literature[5], however, confirms the notion that unless there are data problems, aggregate models are the ones to go for:

STUDIES COMPATING AGGREGATE AND SEGMENTATION MODELS

	Minor data problems	Major data problems
Small or moderate sample (less than 1000 observations)	Aggregate models better 2 No difference 0 Segmentation models better 0	Aggregate models better 2 No difference 1 Segmentation models better 1
Large sample (more than 1000 observations)	Aggregate models better 0 No difference 1 Segmentation models better 0	Aggregate models better 0 No difference 0 Segmentation models better 5

What the preceding table does not show is that although segmentation proved better in five studies where there were big samples and major data problems, the improvements in accuracy – although statistically significant – were small and hardly practically significant. Where the aggregate forecasts were better, they tended to be much better. The sorts of data problems that make segmentation a better bet are interactions and non-linearities. An interaction occurs when the effect one variable has on another depends on the level of a third variable. For example, the effect of price on sales might vary with the quality of the product. For quality products, a high price might increase sales. For poor quality products, a high price might decrease sales.

When it comes to forecasting pharmaceutical sales, such interactions are seldom a practical problem.

There are some circumstances where segmentation is helpful (particularly where you are considering different disease targets - and we will come to this when we consider the techniques that have been proven to work in the real world). We now focus on how the principles of good forecasting apply to segmentation models. Because of the lack of empirical data on segmentation models, this is the one area where it can be difficult to find evidence for all the principles.

How the "six principles" apply to segmentation models

Principle 1: Break the Problem Down

Segmentation forecasting is, by its very nature, a decomposition method. It benefits from spreading the risk and from the cancelling out of compensating errors. It is therefore surprising that it is not more effective.

Principle 2: Be Conservative

Because there is so little empirical data on segmentation forecasting, there is nothing to say about the evidence for conservatism helping. It is reasonable to suppose, however, that as this principle is proven for all other types of forecasting, it almost certainly applies to segmentation forecasting.

Principle 3: Keep it Simple

There are three ways that you can complicate segmentation forecasting. The first is to use an 'indirect approach', the second is to use 'dependent segmentation' and the third is to use too many segments. The first mentioned complication is very common in pharmaceutical marketing. The second is much less common although it has (as you will see) been tried with pharmaceuticals. The third complication is again very common. All three of these complications, however, are likely to lead you to make worse forecasts (as well as costing you a fortune).

Indirect segmentation

The first complication, then, is indirect segmentation.

There are two approaches to segmentation. There is the direct approach. Here you find the segments of customers that are most relevant to predicting change in the thing you are trying to forecast. So, for example, you may find which doctors tend to prescribe more and which less of your type of drug. (Because there is a dependent variable, the statistical techniques used have been called dependence techniques[91]). The most useful technique here is cross tabulations ('cross tabs'). In particular, the most practical technique is simply looking in your prescription audit (or similar) to see who does most of the prescribing.

Then there is the indirect approach. Here you find people who are similar on some causal variables. Then you try to decide how these different groups might behave with respect to the dependent variable. (Because there is no dependent variable, the statistical techniques used here have been called interdependence techniques[91].) The technique most commonly used here is cluster analysis.

It seems fairly obvious that segments chosen because they differ with respect to the thing your are trying to forecast (i.e. the direct approach) will result in better forecasts.

Perhaps because it is so obvious there is little comparative evidence in the forecasting literature (although there *is* some[92]) that a direct approach is better.

There is, however, a total lack of any evidence that the indirect approach works in forecasting. One review was 'unable to find evidence that clustering techniques can improve the accuracy of forecasts'[5].

The indirect approach may at first seem a strange way to segment. It is. But marketing managers allow themselves to be blinded with science by agencies who like to charge a lot of money for these odd approaches.

Dependent segments

The best way to make segmentation forecasting complicated is to assume that the segments affect one another. Academics call this 'dependent segmentation' and it is popular with them. One type of dependent segmentation is 'micro-simulation'. Here the decision processes of various actors in a situation are modelled and changes over time are examined.

> One example in the literature is Amstutz (1967) who developed a microsimulation of the pharmaceutical industry[93]. The various actors interacted in a plausible way. So, if one company increased its promotional spend, others might respond, and so on. Unfortunately (or perhaps fortunately given the difficulty of this approach) there was no evidence that this approach led to better forecasts.

It seems that there is no evidence that the complication of dependent forecasts makes for better forecasts. So, once again the message remains: keep it simple.

Too many segments

In principle, the way we approach a segmentation forecast is like this. Causal variables are proposed that will readily split people so that they behave very differently in terms of the thing you are trying to forecast. (Often, the thing you are trying to forecast is whether, or in what quantities, they will purchase a product.)

The cut-points between segments are somewhat arbitrary. But the following are useful guidelines:

- Select cut-points for which there is adequate data. (One simulation study[94] has suggested at least 10 observations and, preferably, 50 observations.)
- Use cut-points sparingly. Lykken and Rose[95] suggest that you should seldom use more than three. (Using few cut-points is especially important where measurement is poor. If there is a threshold effect, use it as a natural cut-point.)
- In order to segment, we have to decide on some cut-points in the causal variables. If there are threshold levels, these can make good cut-points. Cut-points should be set so that there is good data on segments. If IMS splits out age from 0-12, try not to choose a segment of 0-10. If measurement is poor, use few cut-points. If nonlinearity (interactions) is strong, use more cut-points.

Principle 4: Look at the Problem from Many Angles

There is no direct evidence that combined segmentation forecasts improve accuracy. This may well be because segmentation models are so expensive that there have seldom been two such models looking at exactly the same situation for researchers to combine.

Principle 5: Use Scientific Tools Scientifically

The two problems that you are likely to encounter here are familiar:

Exploratory research

Segmentation is perhaps the area of forecasting – and of marketing – where data dredging is most rampant. There are many powerful computer programs that will allow you to take survey data and find spurious 'relationships' in what is actually background-noise. We have already seen that one technique – cluster analysis – is unhelpful in forecasting. It was criticised then for being an indirect technique. It is also an exploratory technique and as such suffers from all the criticisms of such 'unscientific science'. Indeed cluster analysis manages to combine the worst of all possible worlds: it is indirect *and* it is exploratory.

But an exploratory approach *alone* can be enough to produce meaningless results. One technique that is often used for exploratory direct segmentation is Automatic Interaction Detection (AID).

> Automatic interaction detection (AID) is one of those dangerously powerful techniques often applied with undue caution in market research. The technique automatically splits a population according to the "best" predictor variable (by one way analysis of variance). It then splits the resulting groups again according to the next best predictor variable. And so on. The results resemble a decision tree. Importantly, the AID algorithm does not assume a linear model. So, interactions amongst the predictor variables can be sought out. This increases still further the number of possible patterns into which meaning can be read.
>
> The potential for finding nonsense patterns in the data with AID was demonstrated beautifully in a study by Hillel Einhorn[35]. Einhorn created 1,000 "observations" with the help on a random number generator. Each "observation" had a dependent variable one of ten levels (1 to 10) and ten independent variables each with one of five levels. AID was then run on the data taking sample sizes from 100 up to 1,000 in steps of about 100. AID managed to create highly statistically significant splits in the data ($p<0.001$) with sample sizes of up to 600. Beyond 600 splits with such astounding p values were not possible. In the light of such findings, Einhorn warns that AID should only be used for hypothesis generation. In other words any "patterns" in the data should be replicated in completely new data. Even then at least 1,000 observations are required.

Since their earliest inception AID programmes have taken a step in the right direction in that they now allow the researcher to make more *a priori* input. For example, the researcher can now input decisions on variables and cut-points. Nevertheless, this remains essentially a very powerful (and therefore dangerous) exploratory tool. Scott Armstrong has concluded that 'The dangers of AID may be even greater than stepwise regression because it is so good at picking up spurious relationships'[5].

Even Glen Urban, a pre-eminent management scientist and deft user of statistics, advises that, 'There is no one best or correct way to define market segments. Although statistics can sometimes be helpful, in the end it is a managerial judgement that is needed.'[72]

Forecast uncertainty is always uncertain

There is little or no empirical data to point to reliable ways of assessing the confidence limits to segmentation forecasts. One can systematically quantify subjective estimates - for example by Monte Carlo sampling - but there is no evidence as to a best way or the level of accuracy.

Principle 6: Use Techniques Proven to Work in the Real World

Segmentation makes good sense in theory. It also provides the benefits of decomposition – risk is spread and errors tend to cancel out. Nevertheless, studies using segmentation *as a means to forecast* have been disappointing from the outset.

> For example, one study from the *Journal of Marketing Research* by Imram Currim[96] attempted to use segmentation to predict what type of transport (e.g. auto or bus) people would choose to get from point A to point B. The researcher used two types of segmentation, one split customers into 10 'benefit segments' the other into 9 'situational segments'. But the forecasts generated were no more accurate than a simple aggregate model.

There were some early 'successes' with segmentation, but the successes delivered little of real world value.

> One early reasonably successful use of segmentation was in trying to forecast the number of American families who would try Crest toothpaste in the next year or so[97]. (The American Dental Association had just endorsed Crest because its fluoride helped reduce cavities in children's teeth.)
>
> The market was segmented according to:

- whether Crest offered them a big advantage (because they had children) and if so
- whether they were interested in Crest, and if so
- whether they were venturesome and, if so
- whether they were opinion leaders

> The differences in uptake of Crest between the segments were statistically significant. But*, as is very usual with segmentation exercises, the differences were hardly practically significant.* We would automatically discount households without children - and yet an amazing 39% *did* try Crest. The remaining segments nearly all had virtually the same trial rate (about 50%).

Again and again, this is the problem with segmentation. There is little practical difference between the behaviour of various segments.

The key illustration of how segmentation forecasts make sense in theory but are not practically significant when it comes to forecasting pharmaceutical sales is in benefit segmentation.

Benefit segmentation ought to make a lot of difference in theory, but doesn't in practice.

Benefit segmentation cuts to the heart of product design and marketing.

Two of the leading marketing experts in the US are Glen Urban and John Philip Jones. Urban is the consummate numbers man. Jones is a no-nonsense rule of thumb man. But they both see benefit segmentation as the most important type of segmentation.

Jones: 'the only segmentation of a market that is reasonably common in the real world is one based on *functional differences*. This in turn leads to psychographic and demographic segmentation.' [98] It is easy to see how this is inevitably the case in a pharmaceutical market. If you have a product that is more effective, but less safe than the competition, it is going to be used by more 'aggressive' doctors. But, the starting point is the functional differences between your product and the competition

Urban: 'Segmentation of target groups by their preferences is called 'benefit segmentation'…[It] cuts to the heart of the strategic decision of designing products to meet customer needs. If it can be related to demographic, psychographic, or usage variables, so much the better for targeting of communications and distribution strategies. But even if there is no direct link, benefit segmentation identifies the best positionings for a product or product line.'[72]

The idea that you have to find a part of the market that prefers your product to the competition is so obvious that it hardly warrants saying. And yet identifying those customers or the proportion of the market that they constitute is actually not of much practical significance as far as forecasting is concerned.

There are two reasons. The first is that if you employ a market research agency to do benefit segmentation for you, they will probably use a clustering technique (you have seen the problems with clustering) to do it.

For example, one leading healthcare market research company in the US (they are good and I have used them often) tells us that in theory benefit segmentation is easy[99] and that we should:

- Draw a representative sample of customers
- Measure the importance each customer places on particular product attributes
- Use statistical clustering techniques to group customers with similar wants
- Profile the segments in terms of their demographic, psychographic and product usage profiles
- Name them
- Market to them and
- Develop products for them

But they go on to admit that study after study ends up with the profiles of these ostensibly different customers looking very similar. They use the same products and they have the same demographics[99]

This finding strongly suggests that the segments uncovered are often not 'real' but are patterns pulled out of noise in the sample by the data-dredging computer programs that do the clustering.

My friends in this agency propose a solution [99] the trouble is that they are just more sophisticated forms of data dredging that give you clusters that differ in demographics and product usage. The suppliers guarantee results. And results are assured by the nature of the algorithm used. The trouble is that because the program is even more powerful data dredging, you are, I suspect even more likely to end up with non-existent segments than you were in the first place.

There is a second problem, even if you don't let a market research agency sell you a clustering study and you insist on segmenting according to good *a priori* theory. This time your segments are much more likely to be 'real'. The trouble is that the act of segmenting doesn't give you a very different answer to the one you would get if you didn't segment.

In theory, taking the market as a whole is flawed. If there is a segment that is particularly keen on you product profile you will do disproportionately well there and your overall market share will be higher if you take this heterogeneity into account.

In practice, it makes little difference. To demonstrate this, I created a simulated market place and explored the impact of benefit segmentation. To do this I used the best known technique for relating product profile to market share in pharmaceuticals. (A Pessemier simulation).

In this simulated market place there are (for simplicity of exposition) two products. These two products have two key attributes: efficacy and safety. Product A rates better on efficacy and product B, your product, rates better on safety. Unfortunately for you, most customers say that efficacy is more important than safety. But, for a minority, safety is more important than efficacy.

The results of this market simulation follow. For each scenario we give the results like this:

43% → 42%

Where the percentage before the arrow is the forecast market share using an individual customer level (segmentation) model and the percentage after the arrow is the forecast market share that results if we change to an aggregate level model.

SIMULATION RESULTS WHEN DIFFERENCES ARE EVENLY SPREAD ACROSS THE MARKET (50% PREFER EFFICACY, 50% PREFER SAFETY)

	Realistic importance differences (customers either value efficacy twice as much as safety or visa versa)	Extreme importance differences (customers either value only safety or only efficacy)
Realistic product rating differences (products are twice as good as each other – one on safety, the other on efficacy)	50% →50%	50% →50%
Extreme product rating differences (products are totally superior to each other one on safety, the other on efficacy)	50% →50%	50% →50%

WHEN THE MINORITY IS A LARGE MINORITY (37.5%)

	Realistic importance differences	Extreme importance differences
Realistic product rating differences	47% → 47%	43% → 42%
Extreme product rating differences	43% → 42%	38% → 26%

WHEN THE MINORITY IS A SMALL MINORITY (12.5%)

	Realistic importance differences	Extreme importance differences
Realistic product rating differences	47% → 47%	28% → 26%
Extreme product rating differences	28% → 26%	13% → 2%

In other words it is only when there are unrealistically extreme differences between product ratings <u>and</u> customer importance ratings that market share predictions differ significantly between aggregate and individual level forecasts. Even then, the effects are only really pronounced when we are dealing with a very small minority that holds these extremely different views to the rest of the market.

This simulation demonstrates that – given the margins of error that we are dealing with in new product forecasting – *the differences between individual and aggregate level forecasts are just not important in practice.*

Now, I must stress that the point being made here is that individual (segment) level and average level approaches can often make no practical difference to sales forecasting. That is not to say that the individual level perspective and understanding is not important to the marketing effort.

Here is why. Benefit segmentation makes marketing more efficient, not more effective. A return to the above market simulation can be used to illustrate the point.

Let us focus in on three of the above twelve scenarios. Let us look at where there are realistic product and importance differences and different sizes of minority: no minority (50% prefer our product), a large minority (37.5% prefer our product) and a small minority (12.5% prefer our product). Now, let us look at the proportion of our sales that come from the minority:

PROPORTION OF SALES COMING FROM MINORITY

	Proportion of sales coming from the minority
No minority (50%)	80%
Large minority (37.5%)	71%
Small minority (12.5%)	36%

As your minority gets smaller, the proportion of sales coming from that minority gets smaller. If it is only economical to market to customers who prefer your product, you have problems when the minority that prefers your product is small.

Segmentation by disease *can* be important

The key area where segmentation *is* important and useful in forecasting is by disease. If a product competes in more than one disease area and if the attribute importances are significantly different, it makes sense to segment.

A classic example would be the 'anti-ulcer' market of the 1990's in the US. The US market was a battle ground between H2 receptor antagonists and the more powerful acid inhibitors, proton pump inhibitors (PPIs). In simplistic terms, the main disease areas were peptic ulcers, gastro-esophageal reflux disease (GERD) and gastritis/dyspepsia. In 1993, the current market size for each of these conditions was around 15 million prescriptions per annum. PPIs were gaining just over 5 million prescriptions a year in total and most of these (around 4 million) were coming from GERD. They were, at the time, enjoying strong, double-digit growth rates.

The market growth prospects and the competitiveness of PPIs were crudely as follows:

1990S US ANTI-ULCER MARKET SITUATION

Disease ('segment')	Market growth prospects	PPI competitiveness
Peptic Ulcer	Flat. Eradication of the often-causative bacterium H. Pylori could cure 80%+. Uptake preventing market growth and threatening market decline	PPIs heal more quickly and relieve pain faster.
Gastro-esophageal reflux disease (GERD)	Growing strongly. But, evidence suggesting that up to 50% of cases may be H. Pylori related emerging.	PPIs relieve pain better.
Gastritis/dyspepsia	Flat	The 'milder' H2RAs perfectly adequate (and cheaper)

Clearly very different forecasts are appropriate. Pharmaceuticals analysts rightly forecast that PPIs would continue to grow gaining most of their new business (as in the past) in GERD.

Key questions to ask to determine whether to segment your forecast

In building a vast number of pharma forecasts for major clients, I have learnt that the decision of whether to segment a forecast can best be made by asking the following questions

Are segments of significant size?

We have regularly seen vast spreadsheet forecasting models where 80% of the complexity relates to 5% of the commercial potential. Back-of-an-envelope calculations can usually tell you whether a segment is likely to be commercially significant. (Obviously, the significant size test implies that you should be able to measure the segment and product usage within it!)

Are segments likely to exhibit major differences in product usage?

The only reason for segmenting a forecast is that there are big differences in product usage patterns. The fact that a segment exists is not, of itself, justification for including it in a forecasting model. Generally speaking, product usage differences between segments are less than you might expect. Two examples follow. From the consumer goods sector: Crest toothpaste was launched as child-friendly. And yet uptake levels in families with and without children were not very different! From the pharmaceutical sector: Lipitor was launched as being able to get more patients to target first time. And yet uptakes in new patients and switch patients were very similar.

Are segments distinct from each other?

Sometimes, segments are highly correlated. For example, severe patients and patients receiving, say, third line treatment may largely be the same patients. We only need to consider them once.

In conclusion

Our review of segmentation forecasting has uncovered surprising evidence. Segmentation is seldom of any practical benefit in forecasting. Perhaps, the operating principle for forecast segmentation is best summarized as: "If in doubt, leave it out". Or, to revert to our principles: Keep It Simple!

The key exception is where different diseases are being considered. Whilst the record for segmentation forecasting is disappointing, it does at least make life simpler for us. We can now concentrate on aggregate models, which treat the whole market as one.

Sometimes you do need to significantly segment a forecast – in which case you should perhaps consider getting professional help from, for example, my own company Inpharmation.

Chapter 5: Bootstrapping models – the best way to model the impact of product profiles on sales

Say first, of God above or man below,
What can we reason but of what we know?
Alexander Pope

The first type of forecast that we covered were informal forecasts. The inputs to these informal forecasts were people's judgements. Used in an informal way, judgement was shown to be just about the worst possible way to forecast. But now it is time for judgements to 'rise from the ashes'. For, if properly harnessed through the right type of model, judgements are the most powerful way to model the impact of different product profiles.

67

Introduction to the concept of bootstrapping models

Models that use judgements as their inputs come under the general heading of 'bootstrapping' models. An explanation of why they are called bootstrapping models gives a good introduction as to what these techniques are all about.

The idea that it is possible to build a model of the decision making process that people use to make judgements has been around for a long time. For example, a 1918 paper talks about their use in evaluating job applications[100]. In the 1960's, however, researchers had the idea of using such models as a benchmark for measuring how good judges were at making forecasts. The idea was that the more a judge exceeded the accuracy of a model, the more expert he/she was. But these researchers got a shock.

Reviewing a number of studies in 1974, Robyn Dawes and Bernard Corrigan[101] pointed out that *models of judge's forecasts were meant to 'provide a floor against which the judgement of the experienced [expert] could be compared. The floor turned out to be a ceiling.'*

Since then study after study has confirmed the surprising finding that models of judges forecasts are at least as good as and often better than the best judge[5]. And this is why models of judges' forecasts are called bootstrapping models: judges can lift themselves up by their own bootstraps and achieve better forecasts than the forecasts that were used to build the model.

There are two main types of bootstrapping model: direct models and indirect models. A direct model is built by asking the judge for the rules that he/she uses in making the judgement. For example, if the judge is a doctor forecasting which product profile he/she would prefer, you can ask which product attributes are important and what the relative weightings are. (One example of this technique in pharmaceutical forecasting is 'Pharma Simalto'.)

A simplified caricature of direct bootstrapping follows in case you are not familiar with the technique.

Say you want to forecast physicians preferences for a new drug. Let us just consider two attributes: safety and efficacy. You ask a physician how relatively important safety and efficacy are to him. Let us assume that s/he says:

- Efficacy = 3
- Safety = 2
- Convenience of Administration = 1

Now, for simplicity let us assume that the attributes can be either totally adequate (effective, safe, convenient, scoring 1), or totally inadequate (ineffective or unsafe or inconvenient, scoring 0). We can now predict the ratings that the doctor would give to various drug profiles.

For example, would he prefer an effective and safe drug that is inconvenient to administer or a convenient and safe drug that is ineffective. Our prediction is based on the sum of the weighted product ratings:

Profile	Calculated rating
Effective/safe/inconvenient	3x1 + 2x1 + 1x0 = 5
Ineffective/safe/convenient	3x0 + 2x1 + 1x1 = 3

So, we would forecast that the effective/safe/inconvenient product would be preferred. We could now test the model by giving the doctor these product profiles and seeing if he does rank them in this order.

§

An indirect bootstrapping model on the other hand is built by starting with the judges' forecasts and then working backwards to infer what rules the judge made to make the forecast. For example, if the judge is a doctor forecasting which product profile he/she would prefer, you can ask him/her to choose between a number of product profiles and then run a regression analysis with the preferences as the dependent variables and the various product attribute levels as the independent variables to quantify their impact. The prime example of this technique in pharmaceutical forecasting is conjoint analysis.

A simplified caricature of indirect bootstrapping follows in case you are not familiar with the technique.

Say you want to forecast physicians preferences for a new drug. Let us again just consider three attributes: safety, efficacy and convenience. This time, you give the physician the drug profiles and ask him/her to rate the drugs. Let us assume that he/she says:

PHYSICIAN'S RATINGS OF VARIOUS DRUG PROFILES

Profile	Rating
Effective/safe/convenient	6
Effective/safe/inconvenient	5
Effective/unsafe/convenient	4
Ineffective/safe/convenient	3
Ineffective/safe/inconvenient	2
Ineffective/unsafe/inconvenient	0

Looking at these results, we can now infer that the different attribute levels must have the following contribution (the so-called 'part worth') to the overall rating:

INFERRED PART WORTHS

Attribute level	Part worth
Effective	3
Ineffective	0
Safe	2
Unsafe	0
Convenient	1
Inconvenient	0

We could now use this model to predict the rating that the doctor would give to a drug profile that he has not actually rated. For example, a drug that had a profile of Effective/unsafe/inconvenient would have a predicted rating of 3+0+0 = 3.

The 'importance' of each attribute is the difference between the part-worth for the lowest and highest value for that attribute. So, in this case, the importance of efficacy is 3 (the difference between 3 and 0) and the importance of safety is 2 (the difference between 2 and 0) and the importance of convenience of administration is 1 (the difference between 1 and 0).

In practice a conjoint model is more complex with more attributes and more levels for each attribute. The part-worths are estimated not by inspection but by statistical techniques (such as multiple regression analysis with dummy variables). Nevertheless, it is the same simple concept that underlies the model.

There are half way houses between fully direct and fully indirect bootstrapping methods.

One example is hybrid conjoint analysis. Hybrid conjoint analysis is a technique for obtaining the part-worths of a large number of attributes/levels. Respondents provide direct measures of the importances for features and also provide preferences for a limited number of profiles drawn from a much larger set – a master design. The results are then merged statistically.

§

Another halfway house is preference regression. Here the respondents rate known products on various attributes and then rate or rank these known products. The preference ratings or rankings are then regressed on the product perceptions. Again there are many ways to rate or rank products. Again, operational measures don't make very much difference. Preference regression is simple and intuitive. It may be particularly useful when you have problems categorising products on an attribute because rating is highly subjective. The key problem with this technique however is the 'halo effect' – respondents tend to rate their favoured product highly on everything.

This then is the essence of the bootstrapping approach in both its direct and indirect form. Bootstrapping is subject to the principles of good forecasting. (Indeed it is particularly important that you follow the principles for bootstrapping as agencies have overcomplicated this whole field.)

How the "six principles" apply to bootstrapping models

Principle 1: Break the Problem Down

Bootstrapping techniques are by their nature decompositional. The various key factors that come together to produce the forecast *are* the basic elements of the model.

Principle 2: Be Conservative

Like most forecasting methodologies, bootstrapping models have a tendency to forecast too much change from the current situation. So, conservatism can help accuracy. Say a conjoint model is built and used to try to forecast market shares in a given therapeutic category. There is one incumbent product (with necessarily 100%

market share) and another product is introduced. If the model predicts a 50/50 share for the two products because they are equally preferred, conservatism dictates that we should expect the established product to have a greater than 50% share and the newcomer less than 50% share. This would in fact almost invariably be the case as will be explained (and quantified) later when order of entry models are reviewed.

Pencils and papers or computer screens are not reality. Measures are taken shortly after exposure to the product concept (which is unrealistic) and the respondent may be influenced by the increased availability of the product concept in question. Experience with pre-launch models in the consumer field has led people to down grade "lab measures" accordingly.

> Yankelovich and co-workers used to reduce trial rates by 25% because of lab inflation and then multiply by a clout factor that varied between .25 and .75 depending on introductory marketing spend[102].

Principle 3: Keep it Simple

Academics have had a field day coming up with different ways of constructing bootstrapping models. And market research agencies have made a fortune selling the 'benefits' of the various complex and arcane methodologies.

Many of these methodologies have not been validated and when they have been 'validated', it is generally with holdout tests rather than in the real world. However, the message from a vast literature on the subject is absolutely clear: *it doesn't make much difference which method you use.* Simple methods work just as well as complex methods and direct methods work just as well as indirect methods[103] [104].

No market research conference is complete without unintelligible talks on the benefits of one type of conjoint model over another. Again, all the evidence suggests there is little difference.

> It doesn't matter whether you get respondents to rate product profiles or to rank product profiles. Ranking and rating produce very similar results at both the individual and the aggregate level[105].
> The newer choice based method has been less extensively validated [106]. However, (unsurprisingly) empirical evidence is now emerging that choice based conjoint analysis produces statistically equivalent results to the conventional methods[107].
> §
> When it comes to getting respondents to rate products (indirect methods) or attributes and importances (direct methods), there are different methods you can employ. For example, you can used self rated measures where people are asked to rate, say, importances on, say, a five or nine point scale. Or you can use anchored measures where people are asked to rate the most important attribute as, perhaps, 10 and then others relative to this. Or you can use 'constant sum' scores where people are given, for example, 100 points and asked to share them between attributes. It turns out that it doesn't make much difference what you use. For example, Griffin and Hauser[108] got people to express preferences for seven consumer packaged goods. They used the three types of measure outlined above (self-rated, anchored and constant sum). In all cases preferences among the concepts were highly correlated (Spearman correlations of 0.96).
> §

Recently Professor Henrik Sattler from Jena University conducted a systematic review of head-to-head studies of conjoint (indirect bootstrapping models) and self-explicated (direct models) in the academic literature. His massive review showed that the simple approach was *at least* as effective at forecasting[109].

One reason that it doesn't make much difference which type of model you use is that bootstrapping models have what academics call 'flat optima'. That is to say that weights *near* the optimal values produce almost the same accuracy as those *at* the optimal values[101]…

BOOTSTRAPPING MODELS HAVE 'FLAT OPTIMA'

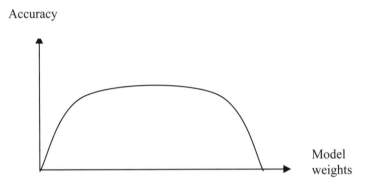

Another reason that it doesn't make much difference which type of model you choose is that many of the different models are complications for dealing with 'problems' that don't have much bearing in the real world.

Perhaps the prime example is 'interaction terms'. In theory, the various product attributes in a conjoint model could interact. For example, safety concerns could be much more pronounced in a product with low efficacy than in a product with high efficacy. It is possible to construct conjoint models that deal with such interactions. (This has been one of the big selling points for a type of conjoint model called 'Discrete Choice Conjoint'.) However, the value of these interaction terms in empirical studies has been marginal[110].

So, use whatever techniques you find simplest.

Principle 4: Look at the Problem from Many Angles

Bootstrapping models generally use the judgements of several – or many – judges. Furthermore, bootstrapping models force the judge to consider all the components of the decision. The most plausible explanation for why bootstrapping works came from Bowman in 1963[111]. He essentially proposed that people have difficulty holding all the elements of a decision in their head at the same time. So, any individual decision is likely to be unduly coloured by the last aspect that was considered. In a bootstrapping model the real impact of each factor is teased out – by taking a number of forecasts into account - and greater accuracy results.

Another way to look at the reason that bootstrapping models work is that there is 'noise' (error) in the human decision making process. By taking lots of judgements the noise is 'filtered out' (compensating errors cancel out) and the 'true' drivers of the decision are revealed[101].

However, in trying to look at your problem from many angles, the key thing to remember when it comes to bootstrapping (and that will probably mean conjoint analysis in pharmaceuticals) is this: *the choice of conjoint method doesn't make very much difference – you will gain far more by looking at your problem from other angles than from worrying about academic debates on which conjoint model to choose.*

Principle 5: Use Scientific Tools Scientifically

A major bootstrapping error is to try to measure the effect of every conceivable attribute. This will result in an unmanageable number of variables with rampant multicollinearity (many of the variables will correlate with each other, so you don't know which ones are really causing changes in the variable to be explained).

This in turn will encourage the use of data reduction techniques like factor analysis. Factor analysis is a generic term that describes a number of techniques that shrink a large number of variables down to a smaller number. These variables are, by construction uncorrelated, so the problem of multicollinearity is apparently solved.

But only apparently. You now don't know what these factors are and you don't know what contribution the 'real variables' make to them (because by construction all the variables that contribute to a factor are highly correlated). Worse still, factor analysis is one of those 'too-powerful' exploratory techniques that can see convincing patterns in noise.

> In one study[112] where workers rated bosses on a number of attributes, important factors were clearly identified. However, the ratings were not really provided by workers but by a random number generator. Given the ability of factor analysis to see sense in noise, it is important to assess the reliability of the factors (i.e. to make sure they are real and are reproduced in similar studies). A review of empirical papers on factor analysis has indicated that a full two thirds of studies make no such attempt[112]. (That is the record for academics who should know better. The record for market research agencies is undoubtedly far worse.)

In fact, if you cannot focus down on a few key attributes for your study, you would be better using direct methods than conjoint methods[72].

Principle 6: Use Techniques Proven to Work in the Real World

Choice of methodology makes little difference

You have seen above that the choice of bootstrapping technique makes little difference in practice. There are two caveats worth bearing in mind.

It makes sense to use an indirect approach when your judges have difficulty articulating their decision making process or where you need good data on a lot of attributes. (The most valid – full profile – conjoint methods can't handle a lot of attributes and anyway if you put a lot of attributes in a conjoint study you are bedevilled by multicollinearity and can't tell which are the really important ones.)

Conjoint models are the most popular indirect bootstrapping method used in pharmaceuticals. Generally there are two methods for data collection with conjoint analysis: full profile and trade off. In the full profile version, respondents have to consider a number of full product profiles. This is inconvenient and restricts the number of attributes to no more than about eight. In the trade off version a subset of attributes are traded off at a time. For example: 'Would you prefer a drug that costs $1,000 and reduces mortality by 5%, or a drug that costs $2,000 and reduces mortality by 6%.' This can be a more user-friendly way to collect data. Unfortunately, there is now a lot of evidence to suggest that the trade-off method is invalid[113] and some evidence to suggest that it is less reliable[114]. You are generally better advised to use a full profile method.

Bootstrapping is useful, but fallible

The fact that different bootstrapping models all tend to produce similar results does not mean that they all provide accurate forecasts. It is naïve and unfair to conjoint analysis to try to predict market share from conjoint results.

As Dick Wittink and Philippe Cattin have pointed out in the Journal of Marketing[115]: 'The closest conjoint studies usually come to validation is by comparing predicted market shares from a simulation for the objects available in the marketplace with their actual market shares. However, for this validation attempt to be meaningful, adjustments should be made for the extent to which respondents are aware of and have access to each of the brands. Such adjustments have been an important feature of simulated test-market model predictions.' Later, you will learn how to combine conjoint (or other bootstrapping techniques with other factors such as advertising weights) to produce more accurate forecasts.

Nevertheless, exponents of conjoint analysis consistently oversell the value of conjoint studies *on their own* as a method for forecasting.

Such overselling has often been done with a quote from Jordan Louviere, Professor of Marketing and Economic Analysis at the University of Alberta in Canada. Professor Louviere is one of the high priests in conjoint analysis. His oft repeated quote is: '[T]here is considerable evidence to support the conclusion that appropriately designed, implemented and analysed conjoint studies can predict the real behaviour of real individuals in real markets.'[116]

Unfortunately, this is the classic quote out of context. For, in the same article, Louviere also points out that: 'Academic research has largely ignored the external validity in conjoint studies…Unfortunately, in most academic studies, conjoint model predictions have been compared with responses to hold-out treatments or their equivalents, or measures of choice intentions, and not actual choices…The majority of writers who have examined the ability of conjoint methods to predict the real choices of real people in real markets have conducted their studies in transport or related contexts…research is needed to determine the appropriate sphere of application of conjoint techniques: that is, in what types of problem are conjoint techniques most and least likely to exhibit external validity?

– and are some conjoint techniques more likely than others to produce externally valid predictions?'

Because bootstrapping models have flat optima (quite large differences in importance weights and attribute ratings have little impact on accuracy) and because bootstrapping models provide an insight into only part of what drives sales and market share (product profile), you can often guestimate the parameters of the model yourself and get results that are just as useful as a full conjoint model. (And bear in mind that a full conjoint model is going to cost up to $100,000 per country.)

We now review such a model.

The InCASE Model: a fast and cost effective alternative to conjoint

The InCASE Model is a cheap and cheerful, direct bootstrapping model for pharmaceuticals. It is part of a forecasting suite called EviCast from Inpharmation. The idea is that you provide the attribute weightings and ratings yourself. (But you can just as easily get a few customers to do it.)

(InCASE is – as you will see – an acronym and is pronounced 'in case')

The reason that we can develop a simple direct bootstrapping model for pharmaceuticals is that, in reality, the key product attributes that drive pharmaceutical preferences are generally the same. (I have spent a fortune of companies' money to find out what in retrospect seems pretty obvious.)

The key attributes are:

- Cost
- Administration
- Safety and
- Efficacy

These four attributes provide the 'CASE' part of our acronym. (We will come to the 'In' part a little later.)

Attribute weights (importances) generally increase as you go down the list and if you guess as follows, you will generally be in the right ball park:

USUAL ATTRIBUTE WEIGHTS

Attribute	Weight
Cost	2
Administration	3
Safety	4
Efficacy	5

Back in 1992 J.J. Bertrand[117] cited the, then, blockbuster drugs and suggested that they each had clear advantages in either efficacy, safety or administration:

BLOCKBUSTERS HAVE CLEAR PRIMARY ADVANTAGES

	Efficacy	Safety	Administration
Zantac		*	*
Renitec		*	*
Capoten	*	*	
Tagamet	*		*
Mevacor	*		
Adalat/Procardia	*	*	
Voltaren		*	*
Cardizem	*	*	
Prozac	*	*	
Naprosyn		*	
Tenormin	*	*	
Ceclor	*		*
Ciprobay	*		
Zovirax	*		
Xanax	*		

These are, of course, the three most important attributes that we use in the InCASE Model

Whilst the relative importance (weight) of the key attributes tends to increase as we go from cost to administration to safety to efficacy, there are exceptions. In particular, there are circumstances where efficacy and safety can be switched. For example, in paediatric conditions, safety is often more important than efficacy. Also, doctors in some countries (notably Japan and Germany) often rate safety higher than efficacy. Our software shows you typical attribute importance weightings from many 'conjoint' studies. These really are very consistent and can be estimated quite well even without surveys.

If you assume these importance levels (weightings) and then estimate the relative ratings of products in your market (say out of 1) you can then perform a weighted sum calculation for each product to calculate its 'score'.

Why can't you simply do this without software?

You can! However, there are three key reasons why software can do a somewhat better job.

The first is that market shares are not directly proportional to the 'preference scores'. If two products have weighted sum scores of, say 2 and 3 this implies market shares in the ratio of 2:3 in other words 40% and 60%. However, the market rewards the better product more (and punishes the inferior product more) than this ratio implies. Hence we need to *exaggerate* the differences. There are a number of ways of doing this (beyond the scope of this book) and software will do this in the most accurate way.

The second reason is that a simple weighted sum calculation does not take into account so-called 'differential enhancement and substitution'. The idea behind this is simple. Say you have three products all with the same preference scores. However, two of the three products have very similar profiles (say "high efficacy/low safety") whereas the third product achieves the same preference score via a very different profile (say "moderate efficacy/high safety"). Now, although there are three products on the market, doctors only really have two performance choices ("high efficacy/low safety" or "moderate efficacy/high safety"). Therefore, wouldn't you expect the different product to get a higher share than the two 'clones'? This is, in fact, what tends to happen and a software program will calculate this effect for you.

Lastly, we come to the 'In' part of the 'InCASE' acronym. Different products have different breadths of indication (In = indications). If a product is indicated for half the number of patients, it may not simply halve this products share potential. The reason is explored below.

Indications supercharge: the final part of the InCASE Model

Indications supercharge means simply this. If there are two competing products that are equivalent in all respects apart from the range of their indications, the product with the broader indications will obtain a larger than expected share.

So, considering two products in a market, one indicated for 100% of possible patients and one for 50%. You might expect the first product to have twice the market share of the second product. But it will tend to have an even greater relative share.

An example of indication supercharge is the battle between Neupogen (G-CSF, Amgen) and Leukine (GM-CSF) in the US. These drugs are colony-stimulating factors that boost the body's production of white blood cells in the bone marrow. Both are effective compounds, but the Amgen product has a slightly less troublesome side effect profile. Nevertheless, Amgen was the first company to obtain an indication for the commercially important use of boosting white blood cell production after the use of cancer chemotherapy. The compound massively outperformed its competitor Leukine in all indications in terms of usage and in terms of physician preference[118]

US PHYSICIAN PREFERENCES FOR NEUPOGEN AND LEUKINE 1995

	Neupogen	Leukine
Prefer product totally	50%	0%
Prefer product mainly	39%	2%

The outperformance was out of all proportion to the modest side effect benefit and is a classic example of indication supercharge.

Again, software can calculate this impact for you.

Case studies using the InCASE Model

Our two case studies to illustrate the InCASE Model focus on first the interferons in the treatment of multiple sclerosis and second schizophrenia treatments. Market share in these markets was unusually dependent on product profile over the time period considered and so these are good candidates for using profile-type models alone.

Our first, InCASE study, then, compares the apparent profiles of two interferons for the treatment of Relapsing Remitting Multiple Sclerosis in the US covering the period up to January 1998.

In the early interferon multiple sclerosis market, the relative benefits of the available drugs were fuzzy and unclear. Trial protocols and biological assays had been different during testing of the products. The relative profiles were hotly debated both by the marketing companies and the neurological community. Indeed, several surveys had suggested that real superiority would be established slowly by feedback from patients in clinical practice[119]. Furthermore important competitors (Teva's Copaxone and Ares-Serono's Rebif) were also nearing the market.

Notwithstanding the uncertainty of the relative profiles, a crude InCASE analysis at the time of the launch of the second interferon, Avonex looked like this:

InCASE STUDY FOR THE INTERFERONS MARKET 1996

Product	Schering's Betaseron	Biogen's Avonex
Ingredients	Recombinant interferon 1b	Recombinant interferon 1a
Introduction	Q3 93	Q2 96
In	Restricted label claiming benefits only of a reduction in annual relapse rate	Broader label claiming efficacy in the slowdown in progression of disease
C	Comparable price	Comparable price
A	Less injections	More injections
S	Apparently more flu like symptoms	Apparently less flu like symptoms
E	Possibly more prone to neutralising antibodies so less effective	Possibly less prone to neutralising antibodies so more effective

We might guestimate the relative attribute weightings and ratings as follows (for each attribute, the best product is rated as 1 and the other relative to this):

INCASE RATINGS FOR THE INTERFERONS MARKET 1996

Product	Weights	Schering's Betaseron	Biogen's Avonex
In	1	1	1
C	1	1	1
A	2	0.8	1
S	3	0.8	1
E	4	0.6	1

InCASE share predictions were:
- Betaseron: 35%
- Avonex: 65%

Just 20 months into the launch of Avonex, (January 1998) the number of new prescriptions for the two interferons were[119]:
- Betaseron: 3,000 (42%)
- Avonex: 4,000 (58%)

Furthermore, looking at the improvement that Avonex seemed to offer one might reasonably expect that if the candidate patient population was not near saturation, the introduction of Avonex might expand the market somewhat. In fact, at the time of introduction, only around 10% of MS patients were being treated. (Strictly, these drugs were indicated only for the 40% of patients who have the 'early' relapsing-remitting form of the disease although a minority of usage was off-label in the 40% of patients who have the other most common form of MS, the 'later' and less-responsive secondary progressive form.)

So, one would expect significant market expansion from a drug that was perceived to be an improved therapy. Indeed, 20 months post-launch, around 15% of MS patients were being treated[119].

It is extremely unlikely that a hugely expensive conjoint study would have given results that were any more meaningful or accurate – especially in such a dynamic market – than this.

Our second InCASE case study looks at another market where product profiles were under the microscope and the key drivers of market share: the US schizophrenia market in the first half of the 1990s.

In the first half of the 1990s, two major new schizophrenia compounds were introduced into the US to compete against the previous gold standard, haloperidole. A crude InCASE analysis would have looked like this[120]:

InCASE STUDY FOR THE SCHIZOPHRENIA MARKET EARLY 90'S

	Haloperidol	Clozapine	Risperidone
In	Schizophrenia	Schizophrenia	Schizophrenia
C	Cheap	Relatively expensive	Relatively expensive
A	2X/day	2X/day	2X/day
S	No agranulocytosis High EPS incidence High other side effects	Some agranulocytosis Low EPS incidence Moderate other side effects	No agranulocytosis Moderate EPS incidence Moderate other side effects
E	High for positive symptoms Low/mod for negative symptoms	High for positive symptoms Mod/high for negative symptoms High for haloperidol refractory	High for positive symptoms Moderate for negative symptoms Unknown for haloperidol refractory

We might guestimate the relative attribute weightings and ratings as follows:

InCASE RATINGS FOR THE SCHIZOPHRENIA MARKET EARLY 90'S

	Weights	Haloperidol	Clozapine	Risperidone
In	1	1	1	1
C	1	1	0.3	0.3
A	2	1	1	1
S	3	0.5	0.6	1
E	4	0.5	1	1

InCASE forecasts were:
- Haloperidol: 7%
- Clozapine: 29%
- Risperidone: 64%

In fact, at the beginning of 1996 market shares were[121]:
- Haloperidol: 9%
- Clozapine: 27%
- Risperidone: 63%

Once again, a useful forecast without the need for an expensive survey.

Our case studies complete the use of the InCASE Model as a means to predict sales with a bootstrapping model alone. (Usually, however factors other than product profile have to be taken into account as well. These are covered in the following chapter.)

The InCASE model can be obtained as part of the EviCast forecasting suite from my company, Inpharmation.

Chapter 6

Chapter 6: Econometric models – the best way to model the impact of marketing variables on sales

Shallow men believe in luck...
Strong men believe in cause and effect.
Emerson

Bootstrapping models, as we have just seen, are the best way to model the impact of *subjective* data (in particular judgements about product profiles) on sales (in particular market shares). Econometric models are models that link changes in *objective* causal factors – like advertising spend – to changes in the forecast variable – like market share.

Introduction to econometric models

Econometric models often use regression analysis to estimate the relationship between causal variables and sales (or whatever) and have been called 'the thinking man's regression analysis'.

Econometric models provide some of the most powerful models in forecasting pharmaceutical sales. They are particularly good at forecasting market shares.

Like all forecasting techniques, the basic principles of good forecasting apply.

How the "six principles" apply to econometric models

Principle 1: Break the Problem Down

To build the best econometric model, you need to find the key causal variables and model each ones impact. Candidates for key variables can be found by expert interviews or brainstorming and the like. Then the many candidates can be culled back to the few that are likely to fulfil the following essential criteria:

- strong causal relationship expected
- causal relationships can be estimated accurately
- large changes (or differences) in causal variables expected (often ignored)
- causal variables can be forecast with *reasonable* accuracy

Principle 2: Be Conservative

The principle of conservatism applies just as strongly to econometric models as to other types of forecast. Indeed, there is even a technical term for applying conservatism to econometric models: mitigation. Mitigation is the application of the 'conservative principle' to econometric models: to the extent that you are unsure of a result, bias your forecasts towards the current situation. In the case of mitigation, this means biasing your forecast towards historic trends and away from uncertain causal relationships.

One way of mitigating an econometric forecast is now covered. You might want to skip this on a first reading.

If we have a simple econometric model in the following form:
$$\Delta Y = a + b\,(\Delta X)$$
Where:

ΔY = change in dependent variable
a = a constant but unexplained trend
b = causal relationship between X and Y
ΔX = change in causal variable

Then, the equation can be mitigated to take more account of the unexplained trend by down-dialling b to $b_{\text{mitigated}}$ such that:
$$b_{\text{mitigated}} = (1/(1+E))b$$
Where:

E is the ratio of the error variance to the true variance.

At the same time, the value of a will have to be increased by a corresponding degree such that

$$a = \Delta Y - b_{\text{mitigated}} \Delta X.$$

In practice, the estimate of E will have to be subjective (i.e. your best guess). But this is better than working with what you believe to be a very flaky model.

At least one study has directly pointed to a improvement in forecasts from mitigation[5].

Principle 3: Keep it Simple

As with other forecasting methods, there seems to be no benefit in complicating things. Indeed, you might even make matters worse as far as econometric models are concerned. A survey of competently performed econometric studies done from an *ex ante* perspective (i.e. the forecasters didn't know the answer when they made the forecast) showed the following:

STUDIES COMPARING COMPLEX AND SIMPLE ECONOMETRIC STUDIES

Study finding	Number of published studies with this finding
Complex studies significantly more accurate	0
Complex studies show trend to more accuracy	4
No difference	0
Simple models show trend to more accuracy	5
Simple models significantly more accurate	2

The above review concluded that: 'this research was hard on me emotionally because it indicated that many of the complex econometric techniques that I had learned were of little practical value in forecasting. Simplicity is a virtue in econometric models.' And concluded that, 'The implication for the analyst is clear cut: use simple methods! In addition to being as accurate, they are less expensive, less prone to errors and easier to implement.'[5]

Having established the general principle that simple econometric models are the ones to go with, we now consider some further applications of the principle.

Simple market share models work best

One of the main uses of econometric models in pharmaceuticals is forecasting market shares. The evidence for econometric models when used to predict market share is consistent with the general finding that simple models are best:

An investigation into the relative accuracy of different market share models in the US showed that no particular functional form was a clear winner. However, simple procedures tended to have the edge. Simple additive models did best in the short term. Simple multiplicative models did best in the long term. Simple ordinary least squares was the best way to estimate parameters[122].

Assumptions matter more than relationships

The thing that most often complicates econometric models is the mathematical form of the relationships between the various variables. But, estimates of relationships are not as important as estimates of assumptions.

In reviewing the record of a quarter century of forecasting experience, Scott Armstrong[33] concluded that: 'A vast amount of research by econometricians has been devoted to finding good ways to estimate relationships [but] forecast accuracy is not highly sensitive to the estimates of relationships. The best advice seems to be to pick a small set of reasonable variables, establish the correct direction of the relationship, and obtain rough estimates of the relationships...far too many resources are devoted to techniques for obtaining better estimates of parameters. Occam's razor should rule: Upon those who advocate more complex procedures rests the burden of proof to show that such procedures are worth the added expense.'

Simple regression analysis is generally all you need to estimate parameters

I said at the outset that econometric models have been called 'the thinking man's regression analysis'. Regression analysis is a simple way to estimate relationships and more sophisticated approaches have not performed well in forecasting.

One more complicated technique, 'ridge regression' was suggested by Darlington[123] in 1978. He seemed to have shown that this more complicated approach beat simple least squares regression.

Technicians leapt eagerly and uncritically on this excuse to make life more complicated and interesting for them. Then, eventually, in 1982, John Morris[124], showed that the original analysis was flawed and that ordinary regression (or even just setting all coefficients to 1) produced better results.

It doesn't make much difference how you measure your causal variables

We noted earlier that the first step in building an econometric model is to select a few key variables. At this first stage, you will be dealing with 'conceptual' variables – for example, you might posit that the level of promotional support is important.

Now you have to turn these 'conceptual variables' into 'operational variables'. An operational variable is one that is defined explicitly, so that someone else could measure it in the same way as you have. You could spend a lot of time agonising over the best way to measure a variable.

Fortunately, the empirical evidence suggests that it doesn't make much difference what operational measure you use.

For example, one study[5] has found that using different estimates of buying power or combinations of the different estimates, made no difference to the accuracy of forecasts.

So, if one of your variables is the level of sales representative support for a product, you could use number of reps detailing or total rep expenditure and not expect your choice of measure to make very much difference to the accuracy of your forecast.

The type of data used doesn't make much difference in practice

There are three basic types of data used in econometric models: time series, cross sectional data and longitudinal data.

In case you are not familiar with what is meant by these terms, an explanation follows.

Time series data takes a given decision unit (e.g. all GP prescribers) and examines differences across a series of time periods. This type of data has been used since at least 1862[125]. It is cheap, fast, realistic and provides a good summary of the current situation. But there tends to be a lack of variation in the data alongside autocorrelation (there isn't much variation in variables from one period to another), interaction (the level of one variable affects the impact of another) and multicollinearity (different causal variables move up and down together, so you don't know which one is having the effect).

Cross sectional data takes a given period of time and examines differences amongst decision units. Now, we tend to see more variation in the dependent and causal variables and there tends to be less multicollinearity and interaction. But, the data tend to be less realistic in predicting the future. (Lab experiments can only be cross sectional.)

Our salvation – in theory - is longitudinal data. Here individual decision units (e.g. individual doctors) are tracked over time. This is the most expensive type of data. It has the big theoretical advantage that each observation serves as its own control and the impact of causal variables should be easier to see.

And yet, what empirical data there is suggests that: 'Overall, the eclectic use of data led to increased costs and provided only small gains in accuracy.'[5]

Non-linear econometric models offer no benefit over simpler, linear models

Perhaps the easiest way to make an econometric model complicated is to make it non-linear. Happily, all useful econometric models either are – or can be transformed to – linear models.

Scott Armstrong[5] says that 'I have been unable to find a published case where non-linear models increased forecast accuracy…[Non-linear models are]harder to understand; they have not been shown to improve our ability to forecast; they are more expensive; and, although not hopeless, they offer little promise for the future.'

Complicating models with feedback loops does not improve accuracy

Econometricians have had fun building models with feedback loops or – as they are prone to call them – 'simultaneous causality'. This happens when say increased sales leads to lower costs which leads to lower prices, which leads to increased sales, which leads to…

Econometricians have tried to find the eventual equilibrium point for this sort of relationship through simultaneous equations. But there is no evidence that they have ever come up with models that help with real world forecasting problems. So, we can keep life simple by not using them[5].

Complicated methods for updating models as more data becomes available do not help accuracy

Once you have built a model, you will want to update it as time goes by and new data becomes available.

Let us say that you build a forecasting model for a completely new model and initially you have no sales data. So, you estimate the parameters (unknown constant terms) in your model by using analogies with other markets. Once you have launched your product, you start to get actual sales data. Now, you have to decide how much weight to give to your analogy and how much weight to give to the small amounts of actual sales data that you have.

The weighting of such new information has provided employment for many econometricians. One technique is Baysian analysis, which provides a formal procedure for updating *a priori* estimates in the light of real world data. This procedure is complex, hard to understand and prone to error. There is no evidence that it provides any advantage over using reasonable judgement[5].

Principle 4: Look at the Problem from Many Angles

Combining simple models that focus on different key variables is more accurate than trying to build one big all-encompassing model.

> One example comes from Namboodiri and Lalu[126] who compared the accuracy of the average of a number of simple regressions to a single multiple regression for 10-year forecasts of population growth. The MAPE (mean absolute percentage error) for the combined forecasts was 5.8 against 9.5 for the single regression.

It seems intuitively obvious that to get great accuracy from econometric models, you need to be accurate in your forecasts for the causal variables. Strangely, it seems that a point is quickly reached where greater accuracy in forecasting the causal variables does not improve accuracy in forecasting the dependent variable. Indeed, generally speaking, unconditional forecasts (where the future values of the causal variables were not known) have tended to be more accurate than conditional forecasts (where the future values of the causal variables were known ahead of making the forecast.)

> A review of studies that compared the accuracy of conditional and unconditional econometric forecasts[33] concluded that: 'Good quality data are often thought essential. However, it has been difficult to find evidence that highly reliable data are needed on causal factors. In fact, contradictory evidence exists. For example, unconditional forecasts (where the causal variables must be forecasted) were found to be superior to conditional forecasts in 10 of 12 published papers.'
>
> This lowering of the quality threshold, however, does not apply to data on the dependent variable[127].

One possible explanation of this phenomenon is that compensating errors in the forecasts of the various causal variables are cancelling each other out.

Principle 5: Use Scientific Tools Scientifically

Two key problems here are again familiar: data dredging and confusing errors in how well past data fits the model with how well future data will fit the model. But, there is a further dimension to the issue of errors in econometric models. One of the big appeals of econometric models is that they let you model the impact of things that are under your control – like the promotional spend. If as a result of your model, you change your plans, your model is likely to now be wrong. But, such an 'error' could be seen as a success. We now cover these three points in turn.

The dangers of exploratory research (data dredging)

The big problem with econometric models comes from running multiple regression analyses on lots of variables and coming up with spurious relationships. Multiple regression on a large number or predictors – particularly when the number of predictors approaches or exceeds the sample size – will result in spuriously high R values that "shrink" when the "relationships" are tested on new data.

> For example, in one reported study[128], 84 predictors were used in a study involving 136 subjects. The initial fit gave a pleasing correlation coefficient, R, of 0.73. But on a new sample, the "relationship" evaporated with R shrinking to just 0.04.

There are even regression programmes that "transform" data (alter the mathematical form of the relationship) repeatedly until a mathematical form is found that provides the best "fit". Again such statistical expediency enormously increases the prospect of finding spurious "patterns" in the data.

> Scott Armstrong[33] in reviewing the successes and failures of forecasting over half a century notes that, 'Stepwise regression and other atheoretical approaches to the development of causal models have produced few successes and many absurd results...*a priori* theory should be used.'

Uncertainty in forecasts is always uncertain (Errors looking back are not the same as errors looking forward)

It is important to distinguish between a measurement model (for assessing historical relationships between variables in the past) and a forecasting model (for predicting relationships between variables in the future).

For example, if more and more hospitals are denying access to reps, response of hospital products to promotion might reasonably be expected to *decrease*.

The standard errors from the measurement model are a starting point in estimating the error in a forecasting model. To these have to be added the errors in estimating initial conditions (perhaps from comparing measures from different sources), the error in forecasting causal variables (perhaps from examining past forecasting efforts) and errors from excluded variables (perhaps best estimated subjectively). It is possible to use Monte Carlo simulation (see Chapter 1) to estimate the likely interplay of these various errors.

When forecast errors are success

Louis Fourt and Joseph Woodlock, point out the catch 22 of econometric forecasting: These models assume no changes in: distribution, promotion, price, product or competitor activity. They also assume that 'the manager does not know the prediction and hence does nothing to alter it. Altered behaviour, of course, is a large part of the value of predictions, and failure for this reason is truly success.'[129]

Principle 6: Use Techniques Proven to Work in the Real World

Ranking data for econometrics

Before we plunge into the details of the best econometric models, it is worth pausing to consider the best sources of data to feed into your models.

There are four sources of data for your econometric models:

1. Historical data
2. Analogy with similar markets/diseases
3. Laboratory experiment/survey
4. Field experiment/test market

The appropriateness of each type of data depends on what you are trying to do.

To establish a baseline (the current situation) to forecast changes from, historic data is the only sensible starting point. Historic data is also useful to estimate small changes. For example, the impact of the third me-too into an established market can be forecast quite accurately using the dynamics that have operated in the past.

For big changes, like the introduction of a new therapeutic category, historic data is of little consequence – particularly if large changes in causal variables have not been experienced. Analogies can be helpful, but have to be handled with great caution. (My favourite example is investors in the Panama Canal who thought that building the canal was a sure-fire money-spinner. They based this on analogy with the Suez Canal – a shipping canal across a small isthmus of land that had made a lot of money. Unfortunately, the analogy was so obvious and so appealing that they did not consider the fact that the Suez canal was built across dessert while the Panama Canal had to be cut through malaria infested jungle. The canal was a commercial disaster. Beware of analogies!) Experiment (ideally field based, but realistically lab/survey based) is the answer.

The following table summarises the circumstances under which it is best to use each type of data:

CHOICE OF DATA TYPE FOR ECONOMETRIC MODELS

Data type	Estimating current situation	Forecasting small change	Forecasting big change	Cost
Historical	***	****	*	****
Analogy		*	**	***
Lab experiment or survey		**	***	**
Field experiment		***	****	*

Failures of econometric models

Before moving on to review the econometric models that work best for pharmaceuticals, it is worth reviewing some very plausible and in some cases popular models that do not seem to work very well.

No life in the Product Life Cycle (PLC) Model

First the Product Life Cycle (PLC) Model holds that sales are *caused* by some internal life cycle. This has been refuted for pharmaceuticals (it has also been refuted for other product types) decades ago.

In 1967 William E. Cox Jr., Professor of marketing at Case Western Reserve University published a seminal study of product life cycles in the pharmaceutical industry[130]. His huge study was based on a sample of 754 ethical drug products in the USA.

Of these products only 313 or 42% achieved what Cox arbitrarily defined as 'commercial birth (new prescriptions of more than 5,000 per month. Those that did succeed did so quickly - with a median length of a month. This lead Cox to conclude that 'an ethical product must quickly establish a market position if it is ever to achieve commercial success'.

For those products that did achieve commercial success, Cox went on to show that for most of them – 70% -, promotional spend is at a peak during the growth phase of the products life cycle. For 25% it is at a peak during the introductory phase and for 5% during the maturity phase. One might conclude that back then, as now, companies put one foot in the water at launch and jumped in with both feet once they had early signs that they were onto a winner.

Cox then went on to study the shape of the product life cycle curves for these products. Only 28% followed the classic 'single hump' curve. The most common curve, occurring in 39% of cases was the 'double humped' curve. Cox attributed the frequency of this shape to the common practice of boosting promotion at the end of the maturity phase of the product life cycle. *In other words the shape of the life cycle was caused by external factors.*

Behavioural models don't behave very well

Econometric models that try to quantify and model the details of human behaviour have not proved very successful. They are not covered in any depth here.

One very plausible behavioural model is the Fishbein Behavioural Model. It says that that the likelihood of a behaviour is the sum of the desirability of various outcomes (e.g. product attributes) discounted by the perceived likelihood of occurring plus the strength with which peers are expected to approve of the behaviour discounted according to the degree that the decision maker cares what his peers think. It sounds very plausible. It looks even more plausible when it is dressed up in the customary mathematics. Unfortunately, empirical studies have shown the Fishbein Model to be of little value. In particular, an attempt to predict prescribing behaviour across a number of pharmaceuticals was a major disappointment with R^2 values around the 0.2 level[131].

No intention of using intention scores

A very significant omission from this report on pharmaceutical forecasting is the use of awareness and intention scores to forecast future sales. Awareness and intention scores are frequently used as a leading indicator of sales in tracking studies. They are in fact very poor predictors of sales and it is important to understand why.

It is ultimately possible to buy awareness for almost any product. (It is much cheaper to get people aware of an appealing product concept, but with enough money and gimmicky adverts, you can buy awareness for the worst dog of a product.)

Awareness, in turn does not correlate with intention to prescribe. (Awareness *does* correspond quite well to a customers consideration set – the products that he/she would think of in a therapeutic category[72]. But products can be in a consideration set because they have been considered and classified as no-hopers, never to be used. This will often be the case if you have bought awareness for an unappealing product concept.)

What if you skip awareness and measure intentions directly. Numerous studies have shown a correlation between purchase intentions and actual behaviour.

> The most famous investigator in this area is Juster[132] who, in a seminal 1964 study tested seven intention measures on 13 products and found that for all measure-product combinations, purchase rate was higher for intenders than non-intenders..
> This type of finding has often been repeated.

But while there is a *correlation* between intention measures and purchases, it is not strong enough or consistent enough to be of very much use in forecasting.

> For example, in 1974, Harrell and Bennett[133] found that the correlation coefficient (r) between intentions to prescribe and actual prescribing behaviour was just 0.37.

What if you skip intention and measure trial purchase. (A trial purchase is the first purchase – or first few purchases – where a consumer buys a product to see whether it is good enough to warrant switching to it.) It turns out that trial purchase is a poor predictor of the eventual level of repeat purchases that build real sales volume.

> It is worth looking at some of the conclusions of J. H. Parfitt and B. J. K. Collins, of the Attwood Group of Companies in the UK, who published the canonical awareness-trial-repeat model for consumer products.
> 'One thing is certain - there is no rule about the level of repeat purchasing to be expected at different levels of penetration.'[90]
> 'In oversimplified terms, persuading the customer to try a brand is a function of distribution, advertising and promotion, but getting her to keep using it is also a function of her acceptance of the product.'[90]
> '[A]ssuming distribution remains fairly constant, the effect of doubling the penetration...could be anything from hardly any increase in ultimate share (maybe from 6% to 6.5%) to a substantial increase (unlikely to exceed a movement from 6% to 9%).'
> '[I]t is comparatively easy, within limits, to influence cumulative penetration, i.e. the number of first-time buyers, but it is extremely difficult to create or influence repeat purchasing for any length of time.'[90]

Don't try to model the unquantifiable

Before leaving the subject of ineffective econometric models, we should mention the legion of ego-sensitive factors that we all feel are important and we all feel we do best. These include:

- Quality of reps and advertising (even experts ratings of ads can't predict sales off-take[98])
- Relationships with key opinion leaders (they'll drop you like a hot brick as soon as a company with "deeper pockets" or a better product comes along)
- Quality of management (the world's greatest investor – Warren Buffet – advises you to sell a company's stock once it starts boasting about the quality of its management).

These things cannot be measured or estimated sensibly. And they are of no impact on your forecasts.

Don't confuse cause with effect

The most important aspects for sales success – as we will see – are being the 'firstest and the bestest'. If you have the best product, many other things follow:

- Formulary listings
- Full distribution
- Favourable notice in guidelines and publications

It is best to keep things simple and model the impact of how good the product is (as we have already done with the InCASE Model) rather than trying to model the impact of such vague forces. In any case many of these 'forces' don't have as much impact as you might expect. Taking guidelines as an example:

The 1990's have been dubbed the decade of guidelines. All sorts of bodies are rushing out to produce guidelines on how every imaginable malady should best be treated. Many of these guidelines are sponsored by pharmaceutical companies who hope that the resulting guidelines will favour their products and that as a result of this they will get more prescriptions. But what is the evidence that guidelines have an impact?

There can be little doubt that the most blue chip set of guidelines is the US's National Institutes of Health (NIH) Consensus Development Program. This programme has put out guidelines on a range of conditions. A major study on the effectiveness of the programme was run several years ago. The results are particularly interesting as the programme was then running at a time when it was less likely to get drowned out by all the other guidelines that have since sprung up.

A telephone survey was used to measure physician awareness both two weeks before a particular conference and then again six weeks after[134]. The results were published in the *Journal of the American Medical Association*, one of the most prestigious, widely read and widely cited medical journals in the US (and indeed the world).

AWARENESS AMONGST PERTINENT SPECIALISTS

	Before	After
Computed tomography	16%	4%
Hip joint replacement	7%	1%

What about when organisations go further and bolster guidelines by linking them to reimbursement? This is what happened with the grandfather of consensus programmes in the 1970's. Then, in a move that pre-dated and presaged managed care in the US, the biggest health care insurance co-operative, the Blue Cross and Blue Shield Association sponsored the 'Medical Necessity Program'. In 1977, the programme identified 42 outmoded diagnostic tests and surgical procedures. Member Blue Cross and Blue Shield insurance plans were advised to withdraw routine reimbursement for these procedures and to require medical justifications from physicians requesting reimbursement.

A review of insurance claims in 1975 and 1978 revealed a 26% decline in listed diagnostic procedures and an 85% decline in surgical procedures. [135] So, even with routine reimbursement withdrawn the impact of guidelines can be very variable.

So much for forecasts that do not work. We now move on to four key econometric models that do work. These are some of the most valuable models available to the pharmaceutical marketer. Three of the models look at the key variables that drive market share within a therapeutic category. One of the models looks at the factors that determine the proportion of patients that are treated by a therapeutic category (in other words how big the market is).

Zipf's Law

The Origins of an Amazing Law

Fifty years ago Professor George Kingsley Zipf of Harvard University wrote a remarkable book. It was called *Human Behavior and the Principle of Least Effort*[136]. In it Professor Zipf showed that many human systems follow the same simple pattern.

The pattern looks like this: the most commonly used word in a book (Zipf used James Joyce's *Ulysses* as one example) is 'the'. 'The' occurs twice as often as the next word, 'of', three times as often as the next word, 'and', four times as often as the next word, 'to' and so on. (Technically, this is one type of 'power law' which means that if the relationship between rank and frequency is plotted on a log-log graph, the result will be a straight line.)

A similar relationship holds for the size of cities. The biggest city in a country tends to be twice as big as the second biggest, three times as big as the third biggest, and so on:

Amazingly similar relationships hold for all sorts of natural phenomena (the size of earthquakes and the size of stock market changes to name but a couple.)

Amazingly, the same law seems to hold – on average – for market shares of similar pharmaceutical products launched into the same market.

Early entry means higher market share for pharmaceuticals

Before moving on to demonstrate how Zipf's Law works for pharmaceuticals, it is worth noting that the fact that early brands get higher shares has been a feature of the pharmaceutical industry dynamics for decades.

A 1970's report for the US government makes this point.

> In 1977, the Federal Trade Commission in the US was concerned by public consternation at wasteful promotion by pharmaceutical companies. It realised however that, despite economic folklore, there was no evidence that harm was being done. So, it commissioned a study[137]. The study looked at a highly competitive, branded market (diuretics) and a less competitive, commodity market (anti-anginals). (How times change!)
>
> They found some support for the economic folklore that markets with high profits tend to have high advertising to sales ratios. However, they noted that the link between advertising and sales is not that simple: 'If firms could increase their profitability merely by advertising, one might logically wonder why all firms do not promote their way to riches. *The road to high profits undoubtedly involves more than the advertising budget.*'
>
> They found that promotional dominance and sales dominance do tend to go hand in hand. However, 'opportunities for gaining sales via promotion are decidedly limited. Large-scale promotion of brands that offer nothing new is likely to go unrewarded.'
>
> And they noted that advertising itself was not a barrier to entry, rather, 'consumers themselves create a barrier by responding to the promotion of early-to-enter brands more favourably than to the promotion of later-to-enter brands.'

This same force is alive and well today in the US and other relatively 'free market' pharmaceutical markets. Indeed, the market's preference for early and innovative products is a spur to innovation. However in highly controlled market the mechanism breaks down stifling innovation. A contrast between the American and Japanese pharma markets illustrates the point well.

> So, in the United States in the early 1990's, over fifteen years after the introduction of major beta-blockers, the first four products to the market still had a combined market share in excess of 80%. In Japan, the first four entrants share rapidly fell to 10% by the early 90s. In the US, only eleven beta-blockers *including generics* were successfully launched up to 1992. Meanwhile, the Japanese market was a maelstrom of exit and entry. Over thirty different molecules had been launched by 1992 and over half of these once successful products were now failures[138].
>
> Physician choice in the US is technology driven, brand loyal and price insensitive. This rewards innovation. Physician choice in Japan is price sensitive, brand-fickle and technology apathetic. This is because so many ineffective medicines are registered and the higher the price and the bigger the discount the better - because Japanese physicians make fortunes as dispensing doctors and pharmaceutical reps have traditionally operated as discount salesmen.
>
> So, while at least some US companies were looking for new therapeutic categories, like ACE inhibitors, Japanese R&D money was being squandered on socially unproductive research into ever more me-too beta-blockers.
>
> The American management professor, Lacy Glenn Thomas concludes in a review of industrial policy and international competitiveness in the pharmaceutical industry that:

'Perhaps the most important historical lesson the United States should keep in mind as it reforms its health care sector is that "producer protection" is a disastrous industrial policy.'[138]

What are the mechanisms for the market preferring early entrants?

There have been two streams of research that have tried to explain why earlier products tend to do better than later products. One stream suggests that early entry *of itself* confers an advantage in the market place.

> For example, a survey has shown that people tend to have a positive image of pioneer brands and that there is a similarity between pioneer brand image and individual ideal self image[139].

The other stream of research suggests that it is not early entry *per se* that leads to greater market share, but rather other factors that tend to be related to early entry. For example early entrants can spend more on advertising, adopt the most lucrative positionings, and benefit from the fact that customers like to stick with a tried and tested product. Evidence for these effects now follows.

> Early entrants can afford to spend more on advertising because they have an established sales base. (The effects of cumulative advertising spend on market share will be covered shortly.)
>
> §
>
> Early entrants can adopt the most lucrative position in the market.
> The first entrant to a market ought to position his drug so that it appeals to as many customers as possible. So, if there is a trade-off between efficacy and side effects, the compromise that induces as many doctors as possible to prescribe should be chosen.
> The second entrant is then better choosing a niche by producing a product that is either more effective (but with more side effects) or with less side effects (but with less efficacy). These are smaller niches than the "central position" adopted by the first entrant. But, the later entrant is better accepting these smaller niches and avoiding damaging head-to-head competition (including price competition).
> This effect is quite strong and can be shown to occur even when customers are evenly distributed in their tastes along the attribute dimensions[140].
>
> §
>
> Early entrants profit from the fact that customers like to stick with a proven product unless there are major benefits to an alternative. So, whilst customers are surprisingly prone to try-out new me-too products[98], unless they prove obviously better than their trusted long-term product, they will tend to revert to the long-term product. This means that, all things being equal, people will prefer a first entrant to an identical second entrant.
>
> §
>
> There are theoretical models that predict that first entrants can command a higher price or - at the same price - a higher market share than followers. These are based on the simple notion that once a customer is familiar with a product, they <u>know</u> it works consistently well for them. They are less certain that a new, untried product will work that well for them. The knowledge and experience they have with the first product is worth something to them[141].
>
> §

A graphic illustration of the idea that me-too brands offer less reason for a doctor to get as excited as the he or she did about the pioneer can be seen in a 1995 *In Vivo* article. The article summarised the strategies that new comers into the human growth hormone market planned: 'The newcomers say they will seize opportunities that haven't been sufficiently addressed by Genentech and Lilly. These include highlighting of the subtle differences among products, introducing devices that ease administration, aggressively seeking new indications, opening distribution channels, and above all pricing.' 'Twas ever so.

This view that it is not being first to market *per se* but the impact of other factors that go with being first that confers an advantage in the market place is known as the 'contingency perspective'. One meta-analysis of order-of-entry studies has indeed indicated that the contingency perspective is the more important factor[142].

Validation of Zipf's Law

Zipf's Law applies across a range of product types including pharmaceuticals and consumer goods.

In consumer markets, even with some degree of functional superiority, the first follower typically achieves 47 to 66% of the pioneers share after three years on the market[143].)

But what interests us here is pharmaceuticals.

A single case study is used below to show how easily Zipf's Law can be applied to forecasting pharmaceutical sales. I have used the pleasingly impressive ACE inhibitors in Japan example. (Please note that the fact that Zipf's Law works so well here contrasts with the earlier assertion by Professor Lacey Glen Thomas that "producer protection" policies in Japan always dull the benefits of early entry.)

The established ACE inhibitors (in order of launch) in 1981 were:
- Captopril
- Enalapril
- Alalcepril
- Delapril

Using Zipf's Law we would expect relative market shares of:

RELATIVE MARKET SHARES FROM ZIPF'S LAW

	Relative share
Captopril	1/1
Enalapril	1/2
Alalcepril	1/3
Delapril	1/4

To determine forecast market shares, we simply calculate the percentage that each relative share constitutes of the total:

ACTUAL MARKET SHARES FROM ZIPF'S LAW

	Forecast share
Captopril	48%
Enalapril	24%
Alalcepril	16%
Delapril	12%

We can now compare this with the actual shares at the time:

COMPARISON OF ZIPF'S LAW FORECASTS AND ACTUAL

	Actual share	Forecast share
Captopril	47%	48%
Enalapril	27%	24%
Alalcepril	14%	16%
Delapril	12%	12%

Now, we can calculate the adjusted absolute percentage error for each product's forecast and, taking the average of these, the adjusted Mean Absolute Percentage Error for the forecasts.

ERRORS FOR ZIPF'S LAW FORECASTS

	Actual share	Forecast share	Adjusted absolute percentage error
Captopril	47%	48%	2%
Enalapril	27%	24%	13%
Alalcepril	14%	16%	16%
Delapril	12%	12%	2%
Mean			8%

Hence, this simple law, in the absence of any knowledge of product profiles or promotional support can at minimal cost and effort provide forecasts that are as accurate as a conjoint analysis study!

This is a single example and that does not constitute a validation study! When we apply Zipf's law to a very large number of pharma categories in many countries we find that it is directionally right (early entry does favour brands) but quantitatively wrong (Zipf's law rewards early entry too much). Nevertheless, by complicating the mathematics a little, we can develop an algorithm ('Modified Zipf's Law) that does very accurately reflect the relationship between launch order and eventual market shares.

**Modified Year 5 Market Share
vs. Modified Zipf's Law**

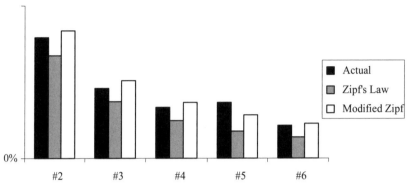

The mathematics involved is beyond the scope of an introductory book such as this. However, you can easily apply it via my company's EviCast forecasting system.

Zipf's law is particularly useful when, order to market is the key factor in your forecasting. For example, if you are developing a compound that is part of a new therapeutic-category-to-be. You don't know with any certainly what the profile of these new agents will be, but you know that a number of companies are in the race. Taking into account the known development stage of your competitors and their expected drop-out rates (about 75% of those in phase I, about 65% of those in phase II and about 30% of those in phase III) you can use Zipf's law to estimate your future market share.

Also Zipf's law is useful as part of a basket of forecasts that you average. (Remember: "look at the problem from many angles".) One of the other angles that you will want to look from in estimating market share is considering product profile. We have already explained how to do this with bootstrapping models and, specifically, the InCASE Model. The other key angle for forecasting market shares is promotional spends. We now consider how to model its impact.

The PACE Model of the impact of promotion on market share

Because pharmaceutical marketers spend so much of their time promoting and advertising their products, they find it hard to accept that dynamic advertising is not the most important aspect of a pharmaceutical brand's success. It is not.

As we will see, product profile and order of entry are the most important factors. Advertising is necessary, but the quantity matters more than the quality.

But the myth of the paramount importance of creative content is widespread

The myth that it is the creative content that is paramount to the success of a pharmaceutical marketing campaign is constantly reinforced by those who have a vested interest in so doing. In particular, the advertising industry constantly bombards us with propaganda to that effect. The propaganda ranges from a constant stream of advertising awards to agency pitches to advertorial copy in the pharmaceutical marketing press.

To cite an example - Jeff Daniels is Creative Director of Pan Advertising. He recently wrote the following totally unsubstantiated assertion in Pharmaceutical Marketing: 'Many factors dictate the effectiveness of a campaign, including media selection, position, frequency, etc. But superior creative work has always been the heart and soul of effective advertising, whether to launch new products or revive ailing ones.

'Since it makes all the difference, the creative process clearly deserves appropriate funding.' [144]

I leave in the last sentence from the quote as it clearly demonstrates the vested interest in propagating this particular myth.

Predicting advertising response

In fact the truth about advertising (and promotion in general) was summed up by Professor John Philip Jones of Syracuse University who said that 'Manufacturers' strategies, in particular those for their advertising, do not have strong force in a world of free choice. They cannot create demand or alter beliefs, although they are quite effective in reinforcing what is there already.'[98]

Advertising and promotion cements the order of entry effects that we have just discussed (reinforcing use of established and familiar products) and it can get people to *try* a new product. But whether they switch to the new product is down to the product, not the advert.

There are measures that can predict whether people will try a product as the result of a particular advert. (Although such detailed tactical marketing issues lie beyond the scope of a book on forecasting.) However, two points must be made. First, a mediocre advert for a product concept that is intrinsically appealing will be more successful than an award-winning advert for an intrinsically unappealing product. Second, adverts get people to *try* products. Product experience gets them to keep using (and adverts can reinforce this.)

Meta-analysis of advertising effects

The traditional way for economists to measure the impact of advertising is to estimate the advertising elasticity of demand. An elasticity of between 0.2 and 0.3 is typical for pharmaceuticals. (An elasticity of 0.2, for example, means that a 1% increase in advertising would result in a 0.2% increase in sales.)

In a meta-analysis of 128 models, the mean short term advertising elasticity was 0.221. The long term effect (i.e. the carry over into outer years) was 0.468 of the short term effect and R (the correlation between short term and long term effects) was 0.783. We will see later that similar elasticities for pharmaceuticals are the norm.

Incidentally, the idea of advertising elasticity of demand implies diminishing returns on advertising. This is because the cost of an additional 1% of advertising (to produce a given response) gets ever higher as the level of advertising increases.

However, this concept of an advertising elasticity of demand will be incorporated into a later model (that looks at product, order and advertising effects *together* in a single model). So, given that forecast accuracy is improved by looking at our problem from many angles, we will here review another model.

Advertising as a capital investment

The PACE model introduced here is an acronym standing for Promotion As Capital Expenditure. The model has its origins in a famous 1993 Harvard Business Review article[145] in which Adrian Slywotzky, a strategy consultant and Benson Shapiro, a professor of marketing at Harvard Business School, proposed a simple but useful idea. Advertising spend should be viewed as a 'capital investment', because it has a long-term impact on sales. Because advertising in earlier years had bought brand loyalty, cumulative advertising spend rather than this years advertising spend should be the focus of our attention.

Slywotzky and Shapiro showed that across a number of markets – beta-blockers, H2 receptor antagonists and also cigarettes, cumulative promotion/advertising and share of new prescriptions (which would ultimately correspond to market share) were correlated. The beta-blocker example is shown in the following graph.

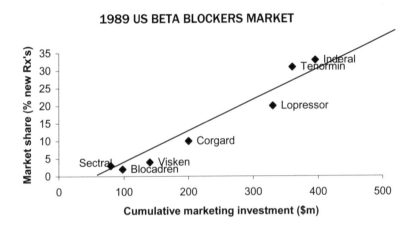

Clearly some products are outperforming (they are above the regression line) and some are underperforming (below the line). The authors suggest that this is because their marketing spend has been deployed 'strategically' by focusing on customers who have low acquisition costs, "switchables", customers generating the most returns "high profit customers" and customers contributing to long term growth "share determiners". (Rather naively, they seem to think that Zantac's success was due to the last strategy with a disproportionate level of marketing effort being deployed on medical students and opinion leading gastroenterologists.)

Nevertheless, this is a useful model. One way of handling the fact that products do not fit precisely along the regression line is to accept that there are external factors causing this (product quality etc) and to adjust future forecasts accordingly. So, if a product is 20% over the regression line future forecast sales are forecast cumulative advertising spend x 120%.

The All-In-One Model of the combined impact of product profile, entry order and promotional spend

Introduction to the All-In-One Model

We have now covered the three most important determinants of market share and looked at models for forecasting their effect:

1. Product profile (Bootstrapping and the InCASE Model)
2. Order of entry (Zipf's Law)
3. Promotional spend (The PACE Model)

One way to estimate the impact of all three factors is to run the three models for your product and take the average forecast. (This is consistent with the principle of looking at the problem from different angles and the benefits of compensating errors). Another approach is to deploy a model that takes all three factors into account. This is what the All-In-One Model – that we are about to cover here – does. (Of course, there is nothing to stop you combining the individual models and the All-In-One Model. Indeed, the evidence suggests that that is exactly what you should do.)

Nevertheless, the All-In-One Model is the single most important and useful model for forecasting pharmaceutical market shares. The explanation that follows here is as simple and intuitive as I can make it. (A user-friendly version of the All-In-One Model is included in Inpharmation's EviCast forecasting program.)

Introduction to the multiplicative model form used in the All-In-One Model

In econometric problems (and in many psychological problems) the multiplicative model is regarded as the gold standard. This is because it is simple and tends to produce good results. This has been apparent for decades.

> For example, O'Herlihy et al.[146] (1967) found the multiplicative model to be superior than the additive model in predicting sales of consumer durables.

There are two things you need to understand about the multiplicative model. The first is why it is called 'multiplicative'. A multiplicative model multiplies the effect of different 'drivers' together. This means that they 'interact' or exhibit 'synergies'. For example, a multiplicative model that had product profile and promotion as its drivers would predict that products with better profiles respond more to promotion (because the two are multiplied together). This is exactly what happens in the real world and may be why such models are more accurate.

The second thing that you need to understand about a multiplicative model is how the impact of each of these factors – product profile, entry order and advertising spend – is determined. It is like this: Each of these factors has an 'elasticity'. The concept of elasticity is best explained with an example. (In fact it is an example that was already given earlier, but it is so important that I will repeat it.) Say advertising has an elasticity of 0.25. What this means is that a 1% increase in the level of advertising will cause a

0.25% increase on the impact of advertising. And because the impacts are multiplied together, it will also cause a 0.25% increase in relative market share.

So – in this example of a multiplicative model – all you need to know to predict products' relative market share is:

1. Measures of product profile, order of entry and advertising spend and
2. The elasticities of product profile, order of entry and advertising spend.

> The mathematics of a multiplicative model are beyond an introductory book like this. However, you can build such a model very easily via the EviCast forecasting system.

The Urban study

The biggest and best review of the impact of product profile, order of entry and advertising spend for consumer products in general was published in 1986 by Glen Urban of the Sloan School of Management at MIT and co-workers[147].

> Urban found that a multiplicative model just like the one described above was the best way to predict the impact of product profile, order of entry and advertising spend on relative market shares. Glen Urban analysed the relationship between order of entry, functional characteristics, advertising and lag between entries. He analysed an initial sample of 82 brands across 24 product categories. These were consumer categories, two of which - analgesics and antacids - were OTC pharmaceuticals. He found a relationship that explained market share very well. But, he had to run a lot of regressions to find it. Under these circumstances, the chances of finding a nonsense correlation that won't work for other products are quite high. So, Urban re-tested the relationship on 47 not previously analysed brands from 12 product categories. It still worked. In fact, Urban found a relationship that could explain 76% of the variation in market shares of the products studied.

All-In-One Model case study: HMG co-reductase inhibitors

We will now review a case study that demonstrates how this model can work for pharmaceuticals in practice. The US HMG co-reductase market of the mid-90s has been chosen because it was a relatively stable market and therefore allowed time for the ultimate market shares predicted by the All-In-One Model to be reached. (We will deal later with how to deal with fast changing markets when we cover diffusion models.)

> The US HMG co-reductase inhibitors market in 1996 was relatively stable and well established. The first product on the market was Mevacor, but the product of choice was the third product Zocor.

US HMG CO-REDUCTASE INHIBITORS RATINGS

	Product profile	Entry order	Advertising (promotion)
Zocor	2	3	4
Pravachol	1	2	4
Mevacor	1	1	1
Lescol	1	4	4

Entering these values into the EviCast All-In-One model produces forecasts of:

US HMG CO-REDUCTASE INHIBITORS FORECASTS

	Forecast share
Zocor	37%
Pravachol	23%
Mevacor	22%
Lescol	18%

The forecast shares alongside the actual prescription shares for 1996 and the adjusted absolute percentage error (aAPE) and the overall adjusted Mean Absolute Percentage Error aMAPE) are shown in the following table:

US HMG CO-REDUCTASE INHIBITORS FORECASTS' ACCURACY

	F/c share	Actual share	aAPE
Zocor	37%	40%	9%
Pravachol	23%	25%	8%
Mevacor	22%	22%	2%
Lescol	18%	14%	21%
aMAPE			10%

Thus, armed with this simple data, we are able to produce a *very* accurate forecast of 'equilibrium market shares' in this unusually stable market place.

Of course, usually, the market is much more dynamic. And we want to know not just the eventual market share, but the year by year market share as new products are launched and enter the fray affecting other products.

To do this we need to create **dynamic** models. In order to achieve this we need to consider the rate at which products trend towards the ultimate shares predicted here. To do this we now need to consider a class of models known as diffusion models. This group of models let you forecast the rate at which products will achieve their market shares. We will cover them in the next two chapters.

We have, so far, focused on econometric models that are useful in forecasting the market share of pharmaceuticals within a therapeutic segment. And these models *are* very useful here. The same models can also be used to make therapeutic classes compete with each other although they are used a little differently. The easiest way to do this is via the EviCast forecasting system.

Using econometrics to forecast diagnosed and treated patients

Econometric models are most often used for forecasting market shares. However, they are very useful for other aspects of pharma forecasting. One example is predicting the proportion of patients with a disease who will be diagnosed and the proportion of these who will be prescribed a pharmaceutical. Getting data on the current state of play can be difficult and expensive. And even if you get current data, it does not tell you what the situation will be in the future when new and better therapies are available.

Fortunately, there are powerful links between a handful of 'drivers' and the proportion of patients diagnosed and then treated for a given disease. My company has collected diagnosis and treatment rates across a vast number of diseases and our EpiTree forecasting support program gives you access to these powerful predictive relationships.

To give you a feel for what they are like, higher diagnosis rates are expected for diseases that are more distressing for the patient; higher prescription rates are expected for diseases for which there are effective pharmaceuticals etc. etc.

EPITREE ALLOWS ECONOMETRIC ESTIMATES OF DX AND RX RATES

Conclusion to econometric models

This concludes our review of econometric models for forecasting pharmaceutical sales. We now have a range of models that are very useful for forecasting market shares and therapeutic category sales levels.

But, the models we have reviewed have forecast the *ultimate* market share or therapeutic category share. You want a forecast of what sales will be *next year and the year after that*, not just some distant eventual market share. And, you need a way of forecasting what will happen to your sales trajectory if circumstances change before the ultimate market share predicted by your econometric model is reached.

To do all this you need 'diffusion models'. These model the spread of a product, or therapeutic category through the user population and hence forecast the shape of the sales curve as it trends towards its ultimate maximum. These are the subjects of the next two chapters.

Because the uptake of "me-too" drugs and innovative drugs are different processes, a chapter is devoted to each. Because there are far more "me-too" drugs than innovative drugs, we start with them.

Chapter 7

Chapter 7: The diffusion of "me-too's"

We are more ready to try the untried when what we do is inconsequential.
Eric Hoffer

Diffusion models try to model not the ultimate level of sales, but the rate at which sales climb to their ultimate level. This happens quite quickly for me-too products, because doctors are not wary about trying something that is not really very new.

An introduction to diffusion models

In essence, all useful diffusion models assume that uptake of a product (or therapeutic category) is due to customers either innovating (using the product because of the information they have received about it) or imitating (using the product because they are impressed with someone else's experience and copying them).

If uptake is due to innovation, then the more people there are to innovate the greater the rate of uptake. At the launch of a new product, no one has yet started using the product, so the number of people available to innovate is at a maximum. Therefore, the *rate* of uptake is at a maximum initially. As more and more people take up the product, the number available to innovate drops and the rate of uptake drops. All of which results in a sales uptake curve like this.

AN INNOVATION ONLY SALES CURVE

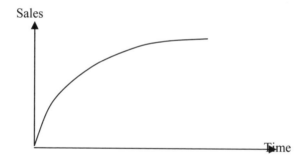

On, the other hand, if uptake is due to imitation, initially there is very slow uptake – there is no one to imitate. As sales build, there are more and more people to copy so the rate of uptake gets faster and faster. Eventually however, the market saturates and so the rate of penetration slows again. All of which results in a symmetrical S-shaped sales curve. (Symmetrical means that the inflection point – the point at which uptake stops accelerating and starts decelerating) is half way up the S-shaped curve.

This shape of curve is shown over the page.

AN IMITATION ONLY SALES CURVE

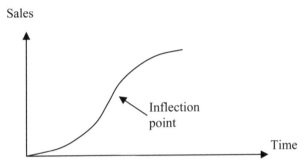

Often, the forces of innovation and imitation are *both* at work. If imitation dominates but there is a little innovation, the rate of initial uptake will accelerate and the inflection point will move further down the S- shaped curve. Like this:

COMBINED INNOVATION AND IMITATION (WITH IMITATION DOMINATING)

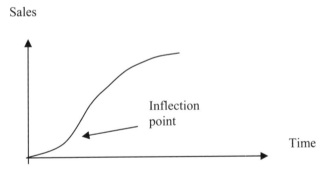

If innovation dominates, but there is a little imitation, a convex curve will result. (Assuming that the rate of innovation is the same, this curve will climb faster than the innovation-only curve – the first curve – because there is innovation *and* imitation.)

Like this:

COMBINED INNOVATION AND IMITATION (WITH IMITATION DOMINATING)

Sales

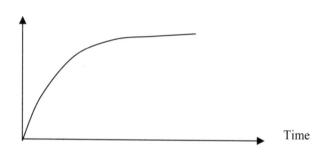

Time

As simple as this all sounds, a huge 'industry' has developed in this area. The diffusion of innovations as a concept became popular in 1962 when Everett M. Rogers published his landmark synthesis in the area. At the time there were just over 400 publications on the subject. By 1995 there were nearly 4,000 studies on the diffusion of innovations[148]. Mathematical modelling of the diffusion of innovations became very popular in 1969 when Frank Bass published details of the most famous diffusion model[149]. The model is now known as the Bass Model. There have been countless variations on this model in the management science literature.

The two types of diffusion that are important in practice for forecasting pharmaceutical sales are the innovation-only model (which is the best way to forecast the progression of market shares for similar products within a therapeutic category) and the combined (imitation and innovation) model (which is best for forecasting the progression of patient pool share for a new therapeutic category). It is the first of these that are covered in this chapter.

Innovation-only diffusion models: an insight into how market shares develop

Most diffusion studies have focussed on major break-throughs. And – as we will cover in great depth later – the spread of seriously novel products is primarily a social process. Most people wait to see how other people get on with the product before taking the plunge themselves (Obviously there have to be *some* innovators or there would never be anyone to imitate.) The pattern of uptake of such major innovations is undoubtedly that of an S-shaped curve and the appropriate model is one of innovation *and* imitation.

Because most diffusion studies have focussed on major innovations and the S-shaped innovation/imitation models that produce them, it is widely believed that the typical sales curve for *all* pharmaceuticals is S-shaped. This is quite remarkable, as this is hardly ever the case. In particular if we plot market share, I have *never* encountered a convincing S-shaped curve for market share progression. There is sometimes a 'restaging' effect where a brand's share is boosted by a major improvement, but this is another issue. Also world wide market share sometimes follows a course that approximate to an S-shape – but this is because of the phasing of international launches.

The myth that all pharmaceutical products constitute major innovations and are taken up as such is widespread.

In his text book *Marketing Strategy in the Pharmaceutical Industry*[150], INSEAD marketing professor Marcel Corstjens asserts that whereas consumer purchases are 'not a major one', pharmaceutical purchases have a 'high risk involved in products'.

Were this generally true, this assertion would be of monumental importance. High risk/high involvement products tend to have a very different buying process and invite a very different marketing approach to low risk/low involvement products. Professor Corstjens does not support his assertion with any evidence, rather he is repeating familiar folk lore. Indeed, most pharmaceuticals are me-too's and these are not viewed by doctors as being particularly high-risk/high involvement products.

The evidence that most pharmaceuticals are me-too's and not break-throughs is common place.

The analysts Lehman Brothers periodically estimate the proportion of the pharmaceutical market that comprises unique products[151]. It is typically around 13-15% of the value market. Given that unique products command a price premium relative to the rest of the market, the volume proportion of products that are unique must be in single figures.

When it comes to assessing the safety of new me-too's, doctors know that the regulatory agencies would not allow them on the market if there were any significant safety issues relative to what went before. So they don't consider most pharmaceuticals as high risk. And, as we shall see, the way that they adopt most new pharmaceuticals and they way that they respond to the promotion of most pharmaceuticals can be understood only if they do *not* view them as high risk/high involvement products.

Another reason that this myth is so pervasive is that one of the first and most famous diffusion studies was on the adoption of a new, breakthrough, high involvement drug[152, 153]. The study showed that uptake was largely a social phenomenon (relying on imitation) and resulted in a familiar S-shaped uptake curve. (We will cover this study and the S-shaped adoption curve for really new products in the next chapter.)

However, subsequent studies of adoption of pharmaceuticals have not confirmed Coleman's findings.

Most notably, Marilyn and Edmund Peay looked at the introduction of temazepam, a me-too benzodiazepine, in Australia in the early 80's[154]. The drug was essentially similar to its predecessors, but had a shorter elimination half-life, minimising the possibility of drowsiness the next day. The Peays found that: 'The main importance of this study is its clear documentation of the relationship between the doctor's favourable reception of temazepam and contact with commercial sources, particularly the detail man, at various stages of the adoption process... Also evident is a general absence of a relationship between reactions to temazepam and involvement in professional activities or within the medical community ... the fact [is] that almost 60% of the doctors named commercial sources as most influential in their first decision to prescribe the drug. [This is consistent with other work that has demonstrated that] under certain conditions, such as where the adoption represents little risk ... the doctor is often willing to relinquish his personal evaluation and prescribe on the information provided by the drug company'

The Peays also cite some other studies that show the same thing and suggest that, **'the failure of these studies to support the Coleman et al findings are the exception rather than the rule.'**

The key seems to be the nature of the innovation concerned. The Peays assert in their paper that 'on average, they [adopting doctors] viewed it as a minor advance. Whereas, Coleman (in the study that found that imitation was important) asserted that the drug was 'a powerful drug, generally used in the treatment of acute conditions'.

Indeed, there is evidence that as the perceived riskiness of a drug increases, doctors take longer to adopt it and rely more on professional, as opposed to commercial sources of information[155].

Now, the first product in a therapeutic class may well be – and usually is – seen by doctors as a high risk, high involvement product. But that product necessarily has a 100% market share. All subsequent products are me-too's. They are relatively low involvement products. Uptake is mainly by innovation. Uptake curves are (as we will see) convex.

In developing models of such uptake curves, the usual principles apply.

How the "six principles" apply to innovation-only diffusion models

Principle 1: Break the Problem Down

You will appreciate that we have now broken the forecasting task down into two stages – ultimate market share (via bootstrapping and econometric models) and the rate at which this share is achieved (via diffusion models). We are also breaking out the uptake of a brands share of its market (therapy class) from the uptake of the therapy class itself (which is covered later).

Principle 2: Be Conservative

The convex diffusion by innovation type of curve is by its nature conservative, trending always towards slower and slower growth.

Principle 3: Keep it Simple

It is possible to complicate things significantly (and this is often done for good reason in consumer goods marketing).

Market share can be broken down into penetration (proportion who have used) x proportion repeat buying x repeat purchase rate (indexed to the rest of the market). This is a good thing in theory (it has all the benefits of decomposition). In practice, the data tends not to be available (or to be very expensive) for pharmaceuticals. Furthermore, there is an important difference between consumer goods and pharmaceutical purchase patterns. Peak purchase rates tend to be reached quickly with consumer goods and more slowly with pharmaceuticals.

The result is that with consumer goods peak purchase rates are reached while there are still many buyers to drop out of the market. This often produces a pattern of sales like this:

SALES PATTERN WHERE PEAK PURCHASE RATE REACHED VERY QUICKLY

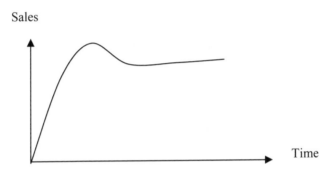

And this justifies a more complicated model for consumer goods.

Whereas with pharmaceuticals, the decrease in users tends to be offset by the increase in purchase rates by the remaining users, giving a sales pattern (as already suggested) like this:

SALES PATTERN WHERE INCREASE IN PURCHASE RATE BUILDS MORE SLOWLY

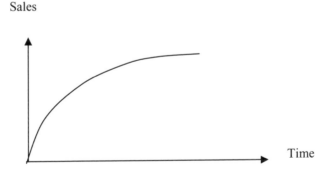

So, the introduction of the above complexities does little to help pharmaceuticals forecasting and is usually unnecessary. Again, as a rule, you should avoid the complexit y.

Principle 4: Look at the Problem from Many Angles

The parameter (constant) for innovation-only diffusion curves (and we will come onto what this is) is best estimated by looking at the problem from a number of angles:

1. The history (if there is one) for the product in question
2. The history of competitor products in the therapeutic category
3. The history of products in analogous therapeutic categories (particularly if there is no history in the therapeutic category in question).

Principle 5: Use Scientific Tools Scientifically

The key point to note here is that the error in how well your diffusion model fits past data is not the same as the error that will be seen with future data. Nevertheless, errors in the future will be highest if we rely on analogies, lower if we have data on close competitors and lowest if we have historical data on our own product.

Principle 6: Use Techniques that are Proven to Work in the Real World

We now focus on a single very simple and very effective model for forecasting the diffusion of me-too product market shares.

The Fourt-Woodlock Model

The simplest – and most useful – innovation-only diffusion model was developed for consumer goods back in 1960 by Louis Fourt and Joseph Woodlock. The model simply assumes that if a product is going to achieve a given penetration, it will achieve a given proportion of that penetration in the first year and the same penetration of the remaining potential in the next year and the same penetration of the remaining penetration the year after that and so on. (As a point of fact Fourt and Woodlock used the model to forecast penetration – the proportion of consumers who had tried the product once. They then complicate their model by introducing the rate of repeat usage etc. As explained above in 'Keep it Simple' this is a necessary complication for consumer goods, but not for pharmaceuticals.)

Thus, knowing just two numbers – the ultimate penetration and the proportion penetrated in the first year – the entire sales trajectory of a product can be forecast. (The proportion penetrated in the first year has since become known as the coefficient of innovation and is generally denoted as p.)

The mathematics to describe this model follow.

The mathematical form of Fourt-Woodlock Model is:
$F(t) = 1 - e^{-(p)t}$
Where:
$F(t)$ = the proportion who have adopted at time t

e = the base of natural logs
p = the coefficient of innovation

The mathematics becomes considerably more complex when you have the real situation of many brands launching sequentially. Nevertheless, we do not have to worry about this here, because simple software, such as my own company's EviCast will do all of this for you.

We now move onto a case study that demonstrates how simply and effectively the Fourt-Woodlock Model can forecast the diffusion of me-too products.

How well does the Fourt-Woodlock model predict brand uptakes?

The Fourt-Woodlock Model predicts brand uptakes rather well (and generic uptakes very well). The following screenshot shows the fit between a Fourt-Woodlock model and the average uptake for nearly 200 pharma brands...

THE FOURT-WOODLOCK MODEL FITS PHARMA BRANDS WELL

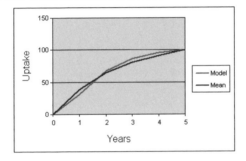

AND GENERIC UPTAKES VERY WELL

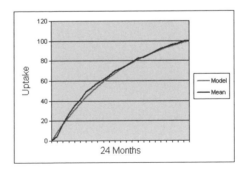

Conclusion to innovation-only diffusion models (for me-too product market shares)

This completes our review of diffusion models for me-too product market shares. As we saw, such products diffuse by a process of pure innovation. Now we move onto products that are genuinely novel. Here, as has already been suggested, imitation is also very important. We now look at how to model such diffusion.

Chapter 8

Chapter 8: The diffusion of break-through products (new therapeutic categories)

When people are free to do as they please,
they usually imitate each other.
Eric Hoffer

Really new products create uncertainly for people. In particular, people are unsure about how a new type of product will work in the real world in the precise circumstances that they face. So, people like to put their toe in the water. They like to test it for themselves. Or, perhaps better still, they like to have someone just like them – a so-called 'near peer' – try it first and tell them how it worked for them. Models for the diffusion of break-through products are based around this fact.

Introduction to diffusion by innovation and imitation models: the key to therapeutic category forecasting

We begin with a very early medical example that show how people will not adopt even promising new ideas without peers to copy from.

In 1601, an English sea captain, James Lancaster, conducted what must be one of the world's first controlled medical trials. At the time, scurvy was the plague of seafarers. On long voyages a huge proportion of a ship's company would invariably fall prey to this syndrome of bleeding gums, easy bleeding, general weakness and ultimately death. But no one knew why. Lancaster set out with four ships on the first voyage of the newly formed East India Company. On his command ship, the men were provided with supplies of lemon juice. The men on the other three ships were not. Most of the men on the treatment ship remained healthy. But by the halfway point on the journey, nearly half of the men on the other three ships had died from scurvy. Many of those remaining were so ill that men from the 'treatment ship' had to be transferred to man the other three ships.

The East India Company were so impressed that they started to issue all their sailors with lemon juice. But not the Royal Navy. It was not until 1747, <u>nearly a hundred and fifty years later</u>, that James Lind, a Royal Navy physician who knew about Lancaster's results conducted another famous experiment. His *Treatise of the Scurvy* provided still stronger evidence that a diet with enough vegetables or fruit juice could prevent the disease. Nevertheless, it was not until 1748 - another forty-eight years - before the Royal Navy adopted this innovation. And it was to take another seventy years until 1865 for the British Board of Trade to adopt the policy and eradicate scurvy from the merchant marine.

In retrospect the slow adoption of what we now know to be a definite prevention of scurvy seems like insanity. And yet, the British Admiralty was not a fuddy-duddy establishment that resisted all change. They snapped up new designs for ships and guns without much hesitation.

So what prevented the uptake of citrus fruits in the prevention of scurvy? This case highlights perhaps the two most important things to appreciate about the uptake of innovations.

The first is that while, in retrospect, successful innovations look like obvious solutions to a problem, initially things usually look far less certain. In this case, there were a number of rival 'cures' for scurvy. Furthermore, Captain Cook's reports from his voyages in the Pacific did not support the notion that citrus fruits could cure scurvy.

The second key point is that when innovations are viewed as representing a significant degree of risk, their diffusion is very much a *social process*. In particular people are impressed by the results obtained by near peers, seeing their usage as being a vicarious trial of the product in circumstances very similar to their own.

So, in the case of citrus fruit and scurvy, it was probably very significant that Lancaster, the original pioneer, was an 'outsider'. He worked for the East India Company and *not* the Royal Navy.

We might expect that a social diffusion process might be important for doctors because cautious uptake of the really new is ingrained in doctors.

As the Lancet has observed: 'The introduction of a new therapeutic agent or interventional technique tends to be viewed with caution, irrespective of the results of earlier studies - "let's wait and see how others find it". Such wary attitudes are instilled early in postgraduate medical training and perhaps reflect a wisdom gained from the experience of promising agents, backed by scientific studies, which on routine use were found wanting.'[156]

What evidence is there that such a diffusion process occurs when it comes to the adoption of pharmaceuticals? Well, for a start, the seminal diffusion study that first suggested that diffusion is a social process, looked at the uptake of a pharmaceutical...

The study was commissioned by the pharmaceutical company Pfizer who wanted to know what the impact of journal advertising was on the uptake of their major new drug tetracycline. Pfizer's parochial question was converted by the three sociologist into a seminal diffusion study.

The study, which was published by Coleman et al in 1957[152], looked at the introduction of the new class of antibiotic in four cities in Illinois in the US in late 1953. (As mentioned, the new antibiotic was tetracycline, but most of the published reports referred to it by the pseudonym 'gammanym'.) The reason that this study is seminal is that the researchers actually used prescription data to determine when doctors really started to use the drug rather than relying on recall as earlier diffusion studies had done.

What the study showed was a classical diffusion process for a risky/high involvement innovation. Knowledge of the drug was spread mainly by the mass media. In this case that meant reps and medical journals. But this was not enough to get most doctors to adopt. Most doctors needed a positive subjective evaluation by a peer to get them started. That process was started off by the few innovative doctors who were prepared to try the drug based on objective data alone. These innovators were more exposed to communication - for example, they attended more out of town meetings. They also tended to be of a higher social status - they treated richer patients and had wealthier practices. And, they tended to be better plugged into the medical social network - all the doctors nominated by three or more colleagues as social friends had tried the drug before the take-off point which occurred in the eighth month of the seventeen month study.

Since this seminal work, a huge body of diffusion studies have been performed. The result is the universal finding that diffusion of innovations is essentially a social phenomenon that occurs through social networks.

And experience with forecasting models of the diffusion process for new product categories also confirms that such diffusion is a social process.

The most famous (and as we will see most useful) such model was created by Frank Bass in 1969. Bass was then a marketing professor at Purdue University. In essence, the Bass Model sees adoption within a population being due to two sources: the mass media and interpersonal communication. People who adopt on the strength of information from the mass media are innovators. People who copy their peers are imitators[149]. The model almost invariably suggests that imitation is more important than innovation [157].

There is other indirect evidence that the diffusion of really new products is a social process. Most doctors do not familiarise themselves adequately with the clinical findings surrounding a new innovation to give them the confidence to innovate.

In 1989, Jean-Pierre Boissel, a French MD and pharmacologist, reported awareness levels for 6 classic and seminal randomised controlled trials (RCTs) that had revolutionised medical understanding on what is the most effective therapy for a number of conditions.

The six studies covered the following:

1. Beta blocking agents in the prevention of late mortality in patients recovering from a myocardial infarction.
2. Prevention of gastric ulcer recurrence by cimetidine.
3. Pentoxifylline efficacy in the treatment of intermittent claudication.
4. Reduction in mortality from breast cancer after mass screening with mammography.
5. The efficacy of long-term anticoagulant treatment in symptomatic calf vein thrombosis.
6. The benefit-risk ratio of clofibrate in primary prevention of ischaemic heart disease.

In a survey of 200 French GP s, the proportion with any awareness of these seminal studies ranged from 2 to 44%. But the percentage of GP s who *actually knew the results* of the studies was uniformly very low and always in single figures. [158]

What makes an innovation diffuse quickly?

Not only is there overwhelming evidence that the diffusion of new product categories is a social process, there is also good evidence as to what makes a product category diffuse quickly and what makes it diffuse slowly. It is important to understand these forces as there are models that allow us to estimate how quickly the process will occur. (We will come on to such models shortly.)

There are five key characteristics that will tend to explain how quickly an innovation is adopted. They are (in order of importance):

1. *Relative advantage* is whether the innovation is better than what is out there already. This can be in effectiveness, economic or even prestige terms.
2. *Compatibility* is the extent that an innovation is consistent with existing values and norms.
3. *Simplicity* is the degree to which innovations are perceived to be easy to understand and use.
4. Trialability is the extent to which innovations can be experimented with on a limited basis. Trialability is particularly important to early adopters, as they have no vicarious experience to draw on.
5. *Observability* is the extent to which the results of an innovation are visible to others.

Innovations that are perceived as being of greater relative advantage, compatibility, simplicity, trialability and observability will tend to be taken up faster and better than those that are not. Research has suggested that is these characteristics of the innovation itself that are the most important predictor of its success. From 49 to 87% of the variance in the rate of adoption of innovations is explained by the above five attributes of the innovation itself[148].

To take an example of a non-pharmaceutical innovation that has been taken up very quickly, think of the mobile phone.

> The mobile phone has clear advantages over a conventional phone - you can use it on the move (and it has snob appeal too!). It is compatible with our telephone culture - it *is* a telephone. It is simple - almost exactly like using a regular phone. It is trialable - most of us got to have a go on someone else's before we got our own. And it is observable - other people benefiting from mobile phones is only *too* easy to observe!

What does marketing have to do to help diffusion?

New categories of product tend to 'take off' after between 10-25% of potential users have adopted. At this critical mass there are sufficient adopters to activate interpersonal networks[148].

If a product offers a big advantage, is simple to use and compatible with current practices, it doesn't need too much help. (There will be more people willing to innovate. You can get them to try such a wonderful product just by giving them samples!)

If the benefits are more ethereal, or if it is difficult to use, requiring a change in practice, it will need a lot of help (and even then might not make it.) Extensive trials can help prime the social system.

> For example, clot-busters were taken up surprisingly slowly even after trials showed unequivocally that they saved lives. The problem was probably that they were not simple to administer and they required a change in the practices of emergency room staff. However, regions where lead hospitals were heavily involved in the trials saw faster uptake, presumably because the social systems were primed.

If your product doesn't offer big advantages, is not simple and requires changes in practices, despair!

> Companies are currently sinking a lot of money into photodynamic therapy for cancer. (This means drugs that make body cells – and particularly cancer cells – sensitive to light allowing them to be destroyed by light – usually with a laser.)
>
> Currently the advantages over surgery are minor. The drugs make patients so light sensitive that some doctors have shifted clinic times to the evening. A lot of hospitals will need new equipment (lasers) to use them.
>
> All the evidence from diffusion research suggests that these drugs are going to have to get *much* better before they take off!

We have now taken a look at some of the evidence for the social diffusion of major new product types and the forces that influence whether and how fast it happens. Now we move onto modelling the process. The models we will cover are of prime importance in forecasting the size of therapeutic categories as a whole. As usual the basic principles of good forecasting apply.

How the "six principles" apply to innovation and innovation diffusion models

Principle 1: Break the Problem Down

The key thing to stress here is that we have now broken down the sales forecast for a pharmaceutical into three forecasts.

1. How many patients are there? (Patient numbers are often quite stable and can be forecast by extrapolation. Alternatively econometric models can be useful.)

2. What proportion of patients will be treated with a therapeutic category? (We are about to cover the diffusion models that are best for this forecast) and

3. What share of the market (therapeutic category) will your product get? (We have covered the bootstrapping and econometric models that are best for this forecast).

Furthermore, the diffusion models themselves break the forecasting problem down. Frank Bass, admitted that: 'Long-range forecasting of new product sales is a guessing game, at best.' But then he went on to point out that, 'Some things, however, may be easier to guess than others.'[149] The models that we will use break the problem down in such a way that we can use the lessons from history when we make our forecasts.

Principle 2: Be Conservative

Because new product categories tend to follow an S-shaped curve, they look early on as though they are following an exponential growth path that is going to take them to dizzying heights.

It is very difficult to forecast when growth will slow and stop, *but it will*. A bias for conservatism will therefore prove useful.

> Forecasting guru Stephen Schnaars advises that 'The risk in growth market forecasting lies at the beginning, not once the market growth is under way. Forecasts have failed far more often than firms that entered later.'[7]

And when markets do mature and level off, they tend to stay that way[98]. The claim made by the cigarette companies that advertising does nothing to alter the overall size of a market *is* largely supported by the evidence. Once the market is saturated with your type of product there is little you can do to change matters. Unless, of course, you significantly improve the product. Even then, the academics still debate whether improving a product's cost-effectiveness will merely speed up adoption[159], or whether it will increase the number of adopters[160].

The message as always: it generally pays to be conservative.

Principle 3: Keep it Simple

The diffusion model that we will cover here is the simplest model that takes into account both innovation and imitation. There have been countless attempts to complicate this original simple model.

> For example, a number of authors have suggested that the influence of innovation and imitation should vary over time. This results in a much more complicated model and it is possible, retrospectively, to find circumstances under which the complications pay off[161]. But there is no prospective evidence that such complications are worth the effort. Indeed there is evidence that the simplest form of the model tends to be more accurate than other commonly used forms of diffusion models, especially when few observations are available[162].

Principle 4: Look at the Problem from Many Angles

New class forecasting is – to reiterate – the high wire act of forecasting. Constantly looking at the problem from many angles and asking the key questions over and over is crucial. Stephen Schnaars[11], one of the leading authorities on forecasting in the US encourages us to:

'Be sure to ask the following questions, which ask most of the basics:

Who are the customers?

How large is the market?

Will the proffered technology offer them a real benefit over existing and subsequent substitutes?

Is the technology cost effective relative to those substitutes?

Is the derived benefit worth the price you will have to charge?

Are cost efficiencies probable?

Are social trends moving towards or away from this market?

Does the innovation require the user to do things differently?

Does the innovation go against customs, culture, or established business practices?'

The models that we will develop here force you to ask these questions – and go some way to helping you find the answers.

On the subject of looking at our problems from many angles – and before we get into our mathematical models – one simple angle that is always worth considering is this. Again and again, in growth markets, the net result of all the dynamics is that new products and categories steal growth from older products and categories leaving the older categories with flat volume and declining share. For example, the number of prescriptions for calcium antagonists remained completely flat from 1994 to 1997 despite the introduction of the AII inhibitors[163].

This provides an extremely simple way of coming at the problem of forecasting therapeutic category sales where existing categories are growing:

Principle 5: Use Scientific Tools Scientifically

Here, once again, we cover two, by now familiar, concepts.

The theory should come before the data

The diffusion models that we use here are consistent with the well-proven theory of how the diffusion process actually works in the real world. Of course, it is possible to be totally empirical and just choose one of the host of mathematical equations that produce complex curves and then fit them to past data. There are many such curves that could be used to model pharmaceutical penetration.

Of course if you use even more complicated equations, you will tend to get even better fits *with past data*. Indeed, the more parameters your equation has, the better you can get it to fit *past data*. The trouble, as always, is that because the relationship has been uncovered by data dredging, there is no reason why it should hold in the future. And it probably won't.

Errors for past data are not the same thing as errors for future data

Remember, new product category forecasting is the high wire act of forecasting. It is very difficult to get it right. As always, the error in a relationship that has held in the past is not a predictor of the error in the future. Your future errors are likely to be greater. Your errors are likely to be much greater early on.

Some authors have pointed out that accuracy increases once you get past the inflection point on the S-shaped curve (the point at which the rate of growth stops increasing – curving upwards - and starts decreasing – curving downwards). Unfortunately, you only know that this has happened in retrospect well after the point has been passed. Other authors have suggested the number of years after which forecasts become more reliable:

Which ever way you look at it, the MAPE (mean absolute percentage error) in diffusion forecasts is high.

In one classic study[164], where accuracy was improved marginally by using a statistical technique called hierarchical Bayes procedures, the mean MAPEs for forecasts just one year in advance were:

- 1-4 years 109%
- 5 years to inflection point 30%
- After inflection point 54%

(These were forecasts for room air conditioners, colour TVs, clothes dryers, ultrasound machines, mammography machines and foreign language programmes.)

The hierarchical Bayes procedure used by the authors works like this. Initially, there is no past data, so you forecast by analogy with other new product categories. As you start to get real sales data for your new product category, you can also forecast by trying to fit a 'Bass curve' to your early sales data. The hierarchical Bayes procedure takes a weighted average of these two forecasts (giving more weight to the method that produces the least variance (highest accuracy) with past data).

The slight improvements in accuracy with this technique have been demonstrated with very sparse data. Although, once again, we see a trend to improved accuracy by taking the average of two forecasts rather than relying on a single forecast.

§

Two well known forecasters Glen Urban and John Hausser advise that, 'The available growth models are effective in predicting life-cycle growth when six or seven years of data are available in the category. Alternatively, an analogy can be drawn to a market where the parameters ... are known.'[72]

§

Your errors are also likely to be greater when the new product's adoption is not straightforward: William Ascher has pointed out that: 'Standardization is least important for innovations that work independently and are not dependent on the common practices of users. Consequently, forecasts for stand-alone innovations have a better chance at success, all other things being equal. Fewer obstacles stand in their way.'[7]

Principle 6: Use Techniques Proven to Work in the Real World

We now move on to identify the models that are proven to work best in forecasting the S-shaped diffusion of new product categories. We start with the simplest possible model for creating an S-shaped curve.

The simplest model for an S-shaped curve: the "imitation-only" logistic curve

The simplest S-shaped curves are generated by models that assume that diffusion occurs just by imitation. (Although there must be some innovation or the process could never get started.) The simplest such model is the logistic curve. Uptake is proportional to the product of the number of users and the number of non-users. Hence it is slow at the beginning (few users) and slow at the end (few non-users) and fast in the middle. This produces an S-shaped curve.

The equation for the Logistic Model is
$$F(t) = 1/[1+(S-1)e^{-pt}]$$
Where:
$F(t)$ = the proportion who have adopted at time t
S = the proportion who have adopted at time 0
e = the base of natural logs
p = the coefficient of innovation

The logistic model works well (and better than more complicated models) for major technological improvements where one technology is completely replaced by another over decades[81]. For example the substitution of cars for horse power in the USA followed a trajectory very close to a logistic curve:

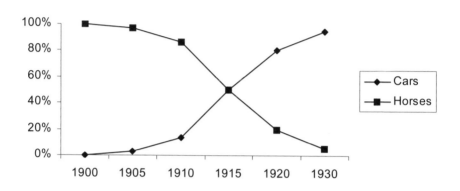

SUBSTITUTION OF CARS FOR HORSES AS PERSONAL
TRANSPORTATION IN THE U.S.

But for pharmaceuticals, there is always an element of innovation as well as imitation. For some therapeutic categories (breakthroughs where the benefits greatly outweigh the costs and risks) this can be very high. Therefore, we need a model that takes imitation into account (like the logistic model just covered) and also takes innovation into account (like the Fourt-Woodlock Model covered in the preceding chapter)...

The simplest model of innovation and imitation: the Bass Model

So, to recap, we have covered the simplest model of uptake by innovation – the Fourt Woodlock Model which simply assumes that a fixed proportion (p, the coefficient of innovation) of those customers that have not innovated do so in each time period.

We have also covered the simplest model of uptake by imitation – the logistic model which simply assumes that the proportion of non-adopters who adopt in a time period is the proportion who have already adopted multiplied by a constant (q, the coefficient of imitation).

A great leap forward was made in 1969 when Frank Bass produced a single model that took both of these factors into account. He did this in the simplest and – with hindsight – the most obvious way: he simply combined the above mentioned two models.

Although the concept behind this model is very simple, the actual mathematical form of the continuous function (to give a smooth line rather than the step-ups in the simplified form above) is rather cumbersome. I strongly recommend that you don't get bogged down with this, but it is included for completeness here.

The mathematical form of the continuous Bass Model is:

$$F(t) = [1 - e^{-(p+q)t}]/[1 + (q/p)e^{-(p+q)t}]$$

Where:

$F(t)$ = the proportion who have adopted at time t
e = the base of natural logs
p = the coefficient of innovation
q = the coefficient of imitation

(An extremely simple and user friendly model of this – and all the other top models covered here – is available in the EviCast forecasting program.)

The Bass Model was not designed to forecast pharmaceuticals –but turned out to do so rather well

Incidentally, the Bass Model was not designed to forecast pharmaceuticals – but turned out to do so. Some background information on the genesis of the Bass Model is included for interest.

In his seminal 1969 paper Frank Bass stressed that his model 'is intended to apply to the growth of initial purchases of a broad range of distinctive "new" generic classes of products[149]. Thus we draw a distinction between new classes of products as opposed to new brands or new models of older products.

Bass tested his model for fit with existing data by regression analysis.: 'The performance of the regression equation relative to actual sales is a relatively weak test of the model's performance since it amounts to an *ex-post* comparison of the equation estimates with the data. A much stronger test is the performance of the basic model with time as the variable and controlling parameter values as determined by the regression estimates.'

By this test, the model worked well at predicting time and magnitude of peak for a range of domestic appliances. But, while the Bass Model was designed for – and originally shown to work well with – one-off purchases, it has since been applied to pharmaceutical sales – most notably by Frank Bass himself. The model is supposed to predict first purchase – not sales of repeat purchase products like pharmaceuticals. So, why does it work? The reason is that sales are proportional to the number of people who have adopted the product. There is a complication, people increase their usage over time. This should skew sales to the right. However, there is another complication, earlier users use more than late users. This should skew sales to the left. It seems that these are compensating errors.

How do we estimate the parameters for the Bass Model?

There are three ways to estimate the parameters for the Bass Model.

Firstly, if there is a well-established sales history, you can analyse past data to find the parameters that provide the best fit. This requires an optimisation program that goes through many iterations to find the best fit. (The EviCast forecasting program will do this automatically for you.)

Secondly, you can use analogies with past products. The general picture from past diffusion studies has emerged from meta-analyses of large numbers of diffusion studies.

In 1990, Professor Fareena Sultan of Harvard University and Professors John Farley and Donald Lehman of Columbia University published a large meta-analysis of diffusion studies[165]. In all, they looked at 213 applications of diffusion models. They were all extensions of the basic Bass Model.

The authors found that for industrial and medical products (such as pharmaceuticals) the average value for p was 0.05 and the average value for q was 0.58.

These are very similar to the values produced by Frank Bass[166] for a range of chronic cardiovascular medications (anti-hypertensives, beta blockers, calcium channel blockers and ACE inhibitors. However – as we will see – more important innovations are adopted more quickly and have higher values for p and q.

Furthermore, these academic studies fail to underestimate the rate of uptake. This is because they do not break down the uptake of a therapy class into its constituent indications. Thus they try to fit a single Bass curve to, say the atypical antipsychotics, without recognising that there are actually multiple Bass curves 'stacked on' each other (psychosis indication, bipolar indication etc.)

Thirdly, you can use simple econometric models that provide links between key uptake drivers and the parameters of the Bass Model. My company has conducted extensive research into this area. The key predictors of pharma class uptakes are:

- The country: some countries are fast (Italy), some are slow (UK)
- The 'therapeutic vacuum' (how much unmet need and how well the new class satisfies it) and
- The fit with prior habits (replacing a tablet with another tablet = fast uptake, replacing a tablet with a complex new mode of administration = slow uptake)

EviCast provides you with a simple calculator based on extensive econometric analysis to estimate how fast your uptake will be.

ECONOMETRIC RELATIONSHIPS CAN GUIDE YOU ON UPTAKE RATES

When therapeutic categories compete

We have now covered the best models for forecasting the diffusion of new product categories. We have covered the simplest and best diffusion model when innovation and imitation are present – the Bass Model. We have also covered four models for estimating the rates of innovation and imitation to feed into the Bass Model.

We now have to face a complicating factor that occurs in the real world. There is often more than one therapeutic category to treat a particular disease. And, these different therapeutic categories can take share from each other.

Fortunately, there are models to deal with this too.

The Law of Capture

Frank Bass has evolved his diffusion model to take account of successive waves of innovation with one generation's diffusion wave washing over and substituting for another[166]

Bass was so convinced that this phenomenon explained the sales pattern in industries where new generations sweep over old - like in computing or pharmaceuticals - that he accorded it the status of a law: the Law of Capture. For, as Bass says: 'the law-like behaviour of demand between successive technologies...are approximately true for every case we have studied'. (Actually, for some of the pharmaceuticals that Bass studied, this so-called law-like behaviour was *very* approximate. We will cover why and what to do about this later.)

The Law of Capture takes a worryingly mathematical form, but the underlying concept is simple: the first class is taken up according to a simple Bass Models and subsequent classes are like waves washing over preceding waves.

For completeness, the mathematical form of the Law of Capture is as follows.

The simplest way to express the Law of Capture mathematically is:

$S_{1,t} = F(t_1)m_1[1 - F(t_2)]$
$S_{2,t} = F(t_2)[m_2 + F(t_1)m_1][1 - F(t_3)]$
$S_{3,t} = F(t_3)\{[m_3 + F(t_2)[m_2 + F(t_1)m_1]\}$

Where:

m_i = the incremental market potential for the ith generation,

t_i = the time since the introduction of the ith generation and

$F(t_i)$ = the proportion of ultimate adopters who have adopted the ith product, as forecast by the Bass Model.

Bass has shown that his Law of Capture Model fits *past* sales patterns well across a range of technologies including some pharmaceuticals (old anti-hypertensives, beta blockers, calcium channel blockers and ACE inhibitors).

For example, this is how it worked for ACE inhibitors, calcium channel blockers and beta blockers in the USA. The period observed is from 1970 to 1987. The line with data points shows the actual and the line without data points the fit with past data and the forecast:

LAW OF CAPTURE APPLIED TO ANTI-HYPERTENSIVES

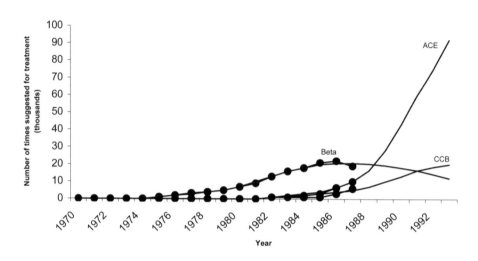

Bass then used the methodology to forecast forward for microchips. Now, in forecasting, he had to guess the future size of the market for the latest generation chip. This was relatively easy because each new generation had increased the market size by a consistent amount. The model forecast 10 periods (quarters) into the future with 'remarkable accuracy'.

Microprocessors are a relatively easy target for the model, because the impact of each new generation is so predictable. Bass then tried to forecast one year ahead using subsets of the data. Bass found that the forecasts were particularly inaccurate early on and when the new generation took only a small share of the market. So the model gave good early predictions for anti-hypertensives but was rather 'unstable' (a euphemism for inaccurate) for beta-blockers calcium channel blockers and ACE inhibitors.

Part of the problem seems to be that Bass made what he admits was a 'very strong assumption' that the values for the coefficient of innovation ('p') and the coefficient of imitation ('q') are the same for each generation. From all that we have seen about the factors that drive the values of p and q this would appear an unwarranted assumption. Indeed, I have achieved better forecasts by estimating p and q separately for each new therapeutic category.

The Law of Contest

Another problem with the Law of Capture is that it assumes that a new generation eventually completely replaces older ones. This happens with computer chips, colour TVs and so forth, but often does not happen with pharmaceuticals. Rather, new therapeutic categories diffuse through the customer base competing with preceding therapeutic categories and taking a share as they go. Indeed, the Law of Capture example shown in the preceding graph shows how this assumption can lead to inaccurate forecasts. ACE inhibitors have not left calcium channel blockers 'in the dust' as the projections suggested would happen.

I have, therefore, found it useful to modify the Law of Capture to allow categories to compete rather than to completely replace each other. I have – rather pompously – called my modified model the Law of Contest. I have done this not because I think it constitutes a law (everything you have read so far has shown you that there is no such thing in forecasting) but to contrast it with the Law of Capture.

The mathematics of the Law of Contest are, again rather tedious. (They are all built into – and are completely 'under the hood' so you don't have to worry about them – the EviCast sales forecasting program.)

> The simplest way to express the Law of Contest mathematically is, assuming a two-product-category system:
>
> $S_{1,t} = F(t_1)m_{max}[(m_1/(1 - m_1))/((m_1/(1 - m_1) + m_2/(1 - m_2))]$
> $S_{2,t} = [F(t_2) - F(t_1)] m_2 + F(t_1)m_{max}[(m_2/(1 - m_2))/((m_1/(1 - m_1) + m_2/(1 - m_2))]$
> Where:
>
> $S_{1,t}$ = the category that has diffused through the smaller proportion of market potential
> $S_{2,t}$ = the category that has diffused through the larger proportion of market potential
> m_i = the market potential for the ith generation,
> m_{max} = the larger of the two product categories' m values
> t_i = the time since the introduction of the ith generation and
> $F(t_i)$ = the proportion of ultimate adopters who have adopted the ith product, as forecast by the Bass Model.
>
> If there are many product categories, the mathematics gets a lot more detailed.

The following example shows how the Law of Contest was used to successfully forecast the convergence of sales of the proton pump inhibitors and H2 receptor antagonists in the US.

If you are serious about accurately modelling therapy class uptakes, you should consider a software solution such as our own EviCast.

Pre-marketing

There is one more concept that can be important in forecasting sales using diffusion models and that is the impact of pre-marketing. The impact of pre-marketing and or clinical trials before a product category obtains marketing approvals can be that some of the adoption process can occur *before the product is launched.*

US ANTI-ULCER THERAPEUTIC CATEGORY FORECASTS
FROM THE LAW OF CONTEST

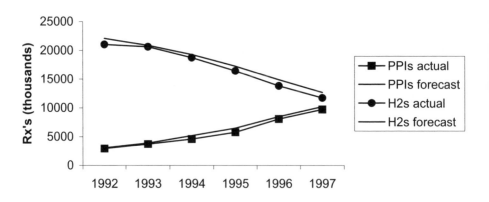

Modeling this is very easy in principle: you simply set time zero to occur some time before launch.

Sometimes, the impact of pre-marketing can be determined by surveys. Sometimes it can be detected indirectly by what is happening in the marketplace as the following example demonstrates.

Obesity is increasingly recognized as having reached pandemic proportions. In the US, for example, more than 20% (40 million people) are obese. And yet in 1994 only around 300,000 prescriptions for anti-obesity agents were written in the US. The reason is that anti-obesity agents were viewed as being ineffective at best and dangerous at worst. Then, in the second half of 1996, Redux (Interneuron/AHP) was introduced. Redux was the first agent with long term clinical data to support it and approval for long-term (up to a year) use. Not surprisingly, the market expanded markedly with the introduction of such an agent. From 1995 to 1997, the number of prescriptions for anti-obesity agents more than quadrupled in the US. Most of the increase happened in 1996, the year in which Redux was launched. But, surprisingly, the steep rise occurred in the first half of the year, before Redux was launched. It seems that pre-marketing increased awareness of obesity and caused the increase in prescribing.

Chapter 9

Chapter 9: Conclusions

The ability to simplify
means to eliminate the unnecessary
so that the necessary might speak.
Hans Hoffman

We have now completed our tour of forecasting principles and methodologies. So, we must summarise what we have discovered. In keeping with one six principles or forecasting, I will try to keep it simple.

The six principles revisited

The principles that we have identified at the beginning have been shown to hold good for every type of forecasting. They must be regarded as elemental components of good forecasting. To reemphasise them one last time:

1. Break the problem down
2. Be conservative
3. Keep it simple
4. Look at the problem from many angles
5. Use scientific tools scientifically
6. Use techniques proven to work in the real world

A decision tree for how to approach your forecasting problem

The techniques that we have covered all have their role. But, in simple terms, a large body of evidence has suggested that you should proceed according to the following decision tree.

Forecasting decision tree

Is a forecast the best way to deal with your business problem? (Maybe not if the possible benefits are much bigger than the possible costs.) Try an *a fortiori* analysis: if you would still go-ahead whatever forecast, why bother?

No   Yes

Use alternatives to forecasting like contingency plans and hedging.

You need a forecast. But have you got enough data to build a model?

No   Yes

You will have to make an informal forecast. You can make it less bad by, for example avoiding biased judges and using techniques like role play where direct questions don't work.

You can build a model. But do you expect things to change in the future (perhaps because you want to change them with your marketing)?

No   Yes

You should consider an extrapolation model. You can make it better by damping the current trend according to how uncertain you are that it is here to stay.

You should build a causal model. But do you expect data interactions?

No   Yes

In such rare circumstances, you should consider a segmentation model. Segmentation models have been a big disappointment. You can make yours even less disappointing by not data dredging.

You should build an aggregate model. The type of model you need depends on the data you have and the problem you face.

To get the most out of <u>subjective</u> data use a bootstrapping model. These models are particularly good at relating product profile to sales.

To get the most out of <u>objective</u> data use econometric models. These models are particularly good at relating entry order, advertising spend to sales and at combining these with product profile forecasts from bootstrapping models.

The key models and their applications

Most of the useful models that we have uncovered are the causal models (down at the bottom right on the preceding decision tree.

We have covered many models. The key models and their uses are summarised in the following table.

KEY MODELS AND FORECASTING CHALLENGE THEY ARE SUITED TO

Forecasting challenge	Appropriate model
Extrapolation of existing trend	Exponential smoothing
Impact of product profile on market share	Bootstrapping models
Impact of entry order on market share	Zipf's Law
Impact of promotional spend on market share	PACE Model
Combined impact of product profile, entry order and promotional spend on market share	All-In-One Model
Therapeutic category share of patient pool	Rx and Dx drivers econometrics
Diffusion of me-too products (in terms of progression of market share over time)	Fourt Woodlock Model
Diffusion of new product categories (in terms of progression of patient penetration over time)	Bass Model
Settings for Bass Model for a particular therapy class/country	Uptake driver econometrics
Impact of therapeutic categories completely replacing each other	The Law of Capture
Impact of therapeutic categories competing and partially replacing each other	The Law of Contest

A note on putting it all into practice painlessly

All of these models are available in Inpharmation's EviCast technology which allows you to insert them easily into your own spreadsheets.

References

What a good thing Adam had –
when he said a good thing,
he knew nobody had said it before.
Mark Twain

This reference section provides you with a complete source guide should you wish to go into any particular topic in greater depth.

1.   Helms, R.B., *Competitive Strategies in the Pharmaceutical Industry*. 1996, American Enterprise Institute.

2.   Carroll, M., *Pharmaceutical Manufacture: The Road from Cost Center to Strategic Weapon*. 1997, Inpharmation: Henley on Thames.

3.   Wheelwright, S.C. and D.G. Clarke, *Corporate Forecasting, Promise and Reality*. Harvard Business Review, 1976. **76**: p. 40pp.

4.   Johnson, G., *The Status of Forecasting in the Pharmaceutical Industry*. 1998, Henley on Thames: Inpharmation.

5.   Armstrong, J.S., *Long Range Forecasting: From Crystal Ball to Computer*. 1985, New York: Wiley-Interscience.

6.   Breckon, W., *The Drug Makers*. 1972, London: Eyre Methuen.

7.   Ascher, W., *Forecasting: An Appraisal for Policy Makers and Planners*. 1978, Baltimore: John Hopkins Press.

8.   Sherden, W.A., *The Fortune Sellers: The Big Business of Buying and Selling Predictions*. 1998, New York: John Wiley.

9.   *The perils of prediction*, in *The Economist*. 1988. p. 71-2.

10.   *Managed Care Spurs Industry Growth*. Scrip, 1997. **2273**(Oct 7th): p. 15.

11.   Schnaars, S.P., *Megamistakes: Forecasting and the Myth of Rapid Technological Change*. 1989, New York: Free Press.

12.   Lynn, M., *Merck v Glaxo: The Billion-Dollar Battle*. 1991, London: Heinemann.

13.   Batson, C.D., *Rational Processing or Rationalization: The Effect of Disconfirming Information on a Stated Religious Belief*. Journal of Personality and Social Psychology, 1975. **32**: p. 176 - 84.

14.   Wagenaar, S., V.d. Heijden, and J.S. cited in Armstrong, *Long Range Forecasting: From Crystal Ball to Computer*. 1985, New York: John Wiley and Sons.

15.   DeSanctis, G., *Computer graphics as decision aids: directions for research*. Decision Sciences, 1984. **15**: p. 463-487.

16.   Lewin, K., *Group Decision and Social Change*, in *Reading in Social Psychology*, T. Newcombe and E.L. Hartley, Editors. 1947, Holt, Rinehart and Winston: New York.

17.   Levine, J. and J. Butler, *Lecture vs. Group Decision in Changing Behavior*. Journal of Applied Psychology, 1952. **36**: p. 29-33.

18.   Bennett, E., *Discussion, Decision, Commitment and Consensus in "Group Decisions"*. Human Relations, 1955. **8**: p. 251-73.

19.   Gregory, W.L., R.B. Cialdini, and K.M. Carpenter, *Self-relevant scenarios as meditors of likelihood estimates and compliance: Does imagining make it so?* Journal of Personality and Social Psychology, 1982. **43**: p. 89-99.

20.   Armstrong, J.S., W.B. Denniston, and M.M. Gordon, *The Use of the Decomposition Principle in Making Judgements*. Organizational Behavior and Human Performance, 1975. **14**: p. 257-263.

21.   Warshaw, P.R., *Predicting purchase and other behaviors from general and contextually specific intentions*. Journal of Marketing Research, 1980. **17**: p. 26-33.

22.	Hacke, J.E., Jr, *The Feasibility of Anticipating Economic and Social Consequences of a Major Technological Innovation.* 1967, Menlo Park, Calif.: Sanford Reseach Institute.

23.	Brody, H., *Great Expectations: Why Technology Predictions Go Awry.* Technology Review, 1991. **7**: p. 41.

24.	Clancy, K.J. and R.S. Shulman, *The Marketing Revolution: A Radical Manifesto for Dominating the Marketplace.* 1993, New York: HarperBusiness.

25.	Dearborn, D.C. and H.A. Simon, *Selective Perception: A Note on the Departmental Identification of Executives.* Sociometry, 1958. **21**(140-4).

26.	Bak, P., *How Nature Works: The science of self-organized criticality.* 1997, Oxford: Oxford University Press.

27.	McNees, S.K. and J. Ries, *How Large are Economic Forecast Errors?* New England Economic Review, 1992(July-August.).

28.	Urban, G.L. and R. Karash, *Evolutionary Model Building.* Journal of Marketing Research, 1971. **VIII**(Feb.): p. 62-6.

29.	Little, J.D.C., *Decision Support Systems for Marketing Managers.* Journal of Marketing, 1979. **43**(Summer): p. 9-26.

30.	Naftulin, D.H., J.E. Ware, Jr., and F.A. Donnelly, *The Doctor Fox Lecture: A paradigm of educational seduction.* Journal of Medical Education, 1973. **48**: p. 630-35.

31.	Armstrong, J.S., *Unintelligable management research and academic prestige.* Interfaces, 1980. **10**: p. 80-6.

32.	Levins, R., *The Strategy of Model Building in Population Biology.* American Scientist, 1966. **54**: p. 421 - 431.

33.	Armstrong, J.S., *The Ombudsman: Research on Forecasting: A Quarter-Century Review, 1960-1984.* Interfaces, 1986. **16**(1): p. 89-109.

34.	Raup, D.M., *Extinction: Bad Genes or Bad Luck?* 1991, New York: Norton.

35.	Einhorn, H.J., *Alchemy in the Behavioral Sciences.* Public Opinion Quarterly, 1972. **36**: p. 367-78.

36.	Mentzer, J.T. and J.E. Cox, Jr., *Familiarity, application and performance of sales forecasting techniques.* Journal of Forecasting, 1984. **3**: p. 27-36.

37.	Little, J.D.C., *Models and Managers: The Concept of a Decision Calculus.* Management Science, 1970. **16**(April): p. 486-485.

38.	Assmus, G., *NEWPROD: The Design and Implementation of a New Product Model.* Journal of Marketing, 1975. **39**(Jan.): p. 16-23.

39.	Armstrong, J.S. and M.C. Grohman, *A Comparative Study of Methods for Long-Range Forecasting.* Management Science, 1972. **16**: p. B281-5.

40.	Danos, P. and E.A. Imhoff, *Factors affecting auditors' evaluations of forecasts.* Journal of Accounting Research, 1983. **21**: p. 473-94.

41.	Murphy, A.H. and B.G. Brown, *A comparative evaluation of objective and subjective weather forecasts in the United States.* Journal of Forecasting, 1984. **3**: p. 369-393.

42.	Strong, L., *Sales Forecasting Comes of Age.* Management Review, 1956. **45**: p. 687-701.

43.	Hauser, P., *Social Statistics in Use.* 1975, New York: Russell Sage.

44.   Dudycha, L.W. and J.C. Naylor, *Characteristics of the Human Inference Process in Complex Choice Behavior Situations.* Organizational Behavior and Human Performance, 1966. **1**: p. 110-28.

45.   Hayes, S.P.J., *The Predictive Ability of Voters.* Journal of Social Psychology, 1936. **7**: p. 183-91.

46.   Kidd, J.B., *The Utilization of Subjective Probabilities in Production Planning.* Acta Psychologica, 1970. **34**: p. 338-47.

47.   Ogburn, W.F., *Studies in Prediction and the Distortion of Reality.* Social Forces, 1934. **13**: p. 224-9.

48.   Hultgren, T., *Forecasts of Railway Traffic.* 1955, National Bureau of Economic Research: Princeton, NJ.

49.   Modigliani, F. and O.H. Sauerlender, *Economic Expectations and Plans of Firms in Relation to Short Term Forecasting.* 1955, National Bureau of Economic Research: Princeton, NJ.

50.   Johnson, G., *Monkey Business: Why the Way You Manage Is a Million Years Out of Date.* 1995, Aldershot: Gower.

51.   Teigen, K.H., *Studies in subjective probability III: the unimportance of alternatives.* Scandevavian Journal of Psychology, 1983. **24**: p. 97-105.

52.   Armstrong, J.S. and T.S. Overton, *Estimating Nonresponse Bias in Mail Surveys.* Journal of Marketing Research, 1977. **14**: p. 396-402.

53.   Huber, G.P. and A. Delbecq, *Guidelines for Combining the Judgements of Individual Members in Decision Conferences.* Academy of Management Journa, 1972. **15**: p. 161-74.

54.   Libby, R. and R.K. Blashfield, *Performance of a composite as a function of the number of judges.* Organisational Behavior and Human Performance, 1978. **21**: p. 121-9.

55.   Hogarth, R.M., *A note on aggregating opinions.* Organizational Behavior and Human Performance, 1978. **21**: p. 40-6.

56.   Kaplan, A., A.L. Skogsta, and M.A. Girshick, *The Prediction of Social and Technological Events.* Public Opinion Quarterly, 1950. **14**: p. 93 - 110.

57.   Stael von Holstein, C.-A.S., *Probabilistic Forecasting: An Experiment Related to the Stock Market.* Organizational Behavior and Human Performance, 1972. **8**: p. 139-58.

58.   Baker, H.G., *Sales and Marketing Planning of the Edsel,* in *Marketing's Role in Scientific Management.* 1957, American Marketing Association: Chicago.

59.   Harris, R.J., *Answering questions containing marked and unmarked adjectives and adverbs.* Journal of Experimental Psychology, 1973. **97**: p. 399-401.

60.   Sigall, H., E. Aronson, and T. Van Hoose, *The Cooperative Subject: Myth or Reality.* Journal of Experimental Social Psychology, 1970. **6**: p. 1-10.

61.   Hofling, C.K., et al., *An Experimental Study in Nurse-Physician Relationships.* Journal of Nervous and Mental Disease, 1966. **143**: p. 171-80.

62.   Rank, S.G. and C.K. Jaconson, *Hospital Nurses Compliance with Medication Overdose Orders: A Failure to Replicate.* Journal of Health and Social Behavior, 1977. **18**: p. 188-93.

63. LaPiere, R.T., *Attitudes vs. Actions*. Social Forces, 1934. **13**: p. 230-237.

64. Schwartz, P., *The Art of the Long View*. 1996: Currency Doubleday.

65. *A perfect day: Peter Schwartz helps people think about the future. But has he gone too far in predicting a 25 year boom?* The Economist, 1998(August 22nd): p. 60.

66. Sudman, et al., *Response Effects in Surveys: A Review and Synthesis*. 1974, Chicago: Aldine.

67. Frederick, W., *Methodological Bias in Public Opinion Surveys*. Public Opinion Quarterly, 1972. **36**(Spring): p. 105-8.

68. Jenness, A., *Social Influences in the Change of Opinion: The Role of Discussion in Changing Opinion Regarding a Matter of Fact*. Journal of Abnormal and Social Psychology, 1932. **27**: p. 29-34 and 279-96.

69. Dalkey, N.C., *Delphi*, in *Long Range Forecasting Methodology*, J.P. Martino and Obereck, Editors. 1967, U. S. Government Printing Office: Washington D. C..

70. Woudenberg, F., *An Evaluation of Delphi*. Technological Forecasting and Social Change, 1991. **9**: p. 131.

71. Dalkey, N.C., *The Delphi Method: An Experimental Study of Group Opinion*. 1969, The Rand Corporation: Santa Monica, CA.

72. Urban, G.L. and J.R. Hauser, *Design and Marketing of New Products*. 1993, Englewood Cliffs, New Jersey: Prentice Hal.

73. Halberstram, D., *The Best and the Brightest*. 1973, London: Barrie and Jenkins.

74. Armstrong, J.S., *Social Irresponsibility in Management*. Journal of Business Research, 1977. **5**: p. 185-213.

75. Gardner, E.S. and E. McKenzie, *Forecasting Trends in Time Series*. Management Science, 1985. **31**(10): p. 1237-46.

76. Schnaars, S.P., *A comparison of extrapolation models on yearly sales forecasts*. International Journal of Forecasting, 1986. **2**: p. 71-85.

77. Lawrence, M.J., R.H. Edmunson, and M.J. O'Connor, *An examination of the accuracy of judgemental extrapolation of time series*. International Journal of Forecasting, 1985. **1**: p. 25-35.

78. Armstrong, J.S., *Forecasting by extrapolation: Conclusions from 25 years of research*. Interfaces, 1984. **14**(6): p. 42-61.

79. Makridakis, S. and R.L. Winkler, *Averages of forecasts: some empirical results*. Management Science, 1983. **29**(9): p. 987-996.

80. Newbold, P. and C.W.J. Granger, *Experience with Forecasting Univariate Time Series and the Combination of Forecasts*. Journal of the Royal Statistical Society, 1974. **Series A, 137**: p. 131-65.

81. Modis, T., *Predictions: Society's telltale signature reveals the past and forecasts the future*. 1992, New York: Simon and Schuster.

82. Ash, J.C.K. and D.J. Smyth, *Forecasting the United Kingdom Economy*. 1973, Farnborough: Saxon House.

83. Brown, R.G., *Less Risk in Inventory Estimates*. Harvard Business Review, 1959. **37**: p. 104-16.

84.   Brown, R.G., *Statistical Forecasting for Inventory Control.* 1959, New York: McGraw Hill.

85.   Hangerman, R.L. and W. Ruland, *The accuracy of management forecasts and forecasts of simple alternative models.* Journal of Economics and Business, 1979. **31**: p. 172-9.

86.   Dalrymple and King, *Selecting parameters for short term forecasting techniques.* Decision Sciences, 1981. **12**: p. 661-9.

87.   Cragg, J.G. and B.G. Malkiel, *Expectations and the Structure of Share Prices.* American Economic Review, 1968. **60**: p. 601-17.

88.   Orson, R.W., *Forecasting in the Electricity Supply Industry*, in *Forecasting and the Social Sciences*, M. Young, Editor. 1968, Heinemann: London.

89.   Makridakis, S., et al., *The accuracy of extrapolation (time series) methods: Results of a forecasting competition.* Journal of Forecasting, 1982. **1**: p. 111-53.

90.   Parfitt, J.H. and B.J.K. Collins, *Use of Consumer Panels for Brand Share Prediction.* Journal of Marketing Research, 1968. **V**(May): p. 131 - 45.

91.   Kendall, M.G., *A Course in Multivariate Analysis.* 1965: Chas Griffin.

92.   Rock, D.A., et al., *A Comparison of Predictor Selection Techniques Using Monte Carlo Methods.* Educational and Psychological Measurement, 1970. **30**: p. 873-84.

93.   Amstutz, A.E., *Computer Simulation of Competitive Market Response.* 1967, Cambridge, MS.: MIT Press.

94.   Einhorn, H., J., *Alchemy in the Behavioral Sciences.* Public Opinion Quarterly, 1972. **36**: p. 367-378.

95.   Lykken, D.T. and R. Rose, *Psychological Prediction from Actuarial Tables.* Journal of Clinical Psychology, 1963. **19**: p. 139-51.

96.   Currim, I.S., *Using segmentation approaches for better prediction and understanding from consumer mode choice models.* Journal of Marketing Research, 1981. **18**: p. 301-9.

97.   Montgomery, D.B. and J.S. Armstrong, *Consumer Response to a Legitimated Brand Appeal*, in *Insights into Consumer Behavior*, J. Arndt, Editor. 1968, Allyn and Bacon: Boston.

98.   Jones, J.P., *What's in a Name? Advertising and the Concept of Brands.* 1986, Lexington, Massachusetts.: Lexington Books.

99.   Morton, J., *Predictive Segmentation Revolutionizes Market Segmentation Research.* A Total View: The Newsletter of Marketing Research Methods, 1988. **1**(44): p. 1-4.

100.   Thorndike, E.L., *Fundamental theorems in judging men.* Journal of Applied Psychology, 1918. **2**: p. 67-76.

101.   Dawes, R.M. and B. Corrigan, *Linear Models in Decision Making.* Psychological Bulletin, 81 (2): 95-106., 1974. **81**(2): p. 95-106.

102.   Yankelovich, s. and White, *LTM Estimating Proceedures.* 1970, New York: Yankelovich, Skelly and White.

103. Akaah, A.P. and P.K. Korgaonkar, *An Empirical Comparison of the Predictive Validity of Self-Explicated, Huber-Hybrid, Traditional Conjoint, and Hybrid Conjoint Models.* Journal of Marketing Research, 1983. **20**: p. 187-97.

104. Leigh, T.W., D.B. MacKay, and J.O. Summers, *Reliability and Validity of Self-Explicated Weights: A Comparison.* Journal of Marketing Research, 1984(August): p. 313-22.

105. Green, P.E. and V. Srinivasan, *Conjoint Analysis in Consumer Research: Issues and Outlook.* Journal of Consumer Research, 1978. **5**: p. 103-123.

106. Elrod, T. and et al., *An Empirical Comparison of Ratings-Based and Choice Based Conjoint Models.* Journal of Marketing Research, 1992. **XXIX**(August): p. 368-77.

107. Louviere, J.J. and G.J. Gaeth, *A comparison of rating and choice responses in conjoint tasks.* 1996.

108. Griffin, A.J. and J.R. Hauser, *The Voice of the Customer.* Marketing Science, 1993. **12**(1).

109. Sattler, H. and Hensel_Borner, *A comparison of conjoint measurement with self-explicated approaches,* in *Conjoint Measurement: Methods and Applications,* A. Gustafsson, A. Herrmann, and F. Huber, Editors. 2001, Springer-Verlag Berlin: Heidelberg.

110. Neslin, S.A., *Linking Product Features to Perceptions: Self Stated Versus Statistically Revealed Importance Weights.* Journal of Marketing Research, 1981. **18**: p. 80-6.

111. Bowman, E.H., *Consistency and optimality in managerial decision making.* Management Science, 1963. **9**: p. 310-21.

112. Armstrong, J.S. and P. Soelberg, *On the Interpretation of Factor Analysis.* Psychological Bulletin, 1968. **68**: p. 430-45.

113. Safizadeh, M.H., *The Internal Validity of the Trade-Off Method of Conjoint Analysis.* Decision Sciences, 1989. **20**(3): p. 451-61.

114. Segal, M.N., *Reliability of Conjoint Analysis: Contrasting Data Collection Proceedures.* Journal of Marketing Research, 1982. **XIX**(Feb): p. 139-43.

115. Wittink, D.R. and P. Cattin, *Commercial Use of Conjoint Analysis: An Update.* Journal of Marketing, 1989. **53**(July): p. 91-6.

116. Louviere, J.L., *Conjoint Analysis Modelling of Stated Preferences: A Review of Theory, Methods, Recent Developments and External Validity.* Journal of Transport Economics and Policy, 1988. **1**: p. 92-119.

117. Bertrand, J.J. *Blockbusters have clear primary selling advantages.* in *World Pharma Conference.* 1992. London: Coopers and Lybrand.

118. Ho, M., *Amgen Inc.* 1995, Goldman Sachs.

119. Tracey, M., J.A. Murphy, and J. Henderson, *Navigating New Waters.* 1998, Goldman Sachs Investment Research: Switzerland.

120. Hecht, E.M., P.A. Brook, and G.M. Reicin, *Schizophrenia: The Next Major CNS Opportunity.* 1996, Morgan Stanley.

121. Ryan, B.A., M. Goldstein, and B.A. Cariello, *Eli Lilly and Company: Setting the Stage for Long Term Growth.* 1996, Alex Brown: Baltimore.

122. Ghosh, A., S. Neslin, and R. Shoemaker, *A Comparison of Market Share Models and Estimation Proceedures.* Journal of Marketing Research, 1984. **16**: p. 202-10.

123. Darlington, R.B., *Reduced variance regression.* Psychological Bulletin, 1978. **85**: p. 1238-1255.

124. Morris, J.D., *Ridge regression and some alternative weighting techniques: A comment on Darlington.* Psychological Bulletin, 1982. **91**: p. 203-210.

125. Zarnowitz, V., *Prediction and Forecasting, Economic.* International Encyclopedia of the Social Sciences, 1968. **12**: p. 425-439.

126. Namboodiri, N.K. and N.M. Lalu, *The Average of Several Simple Regression Estimates as an Alternative to the Multiple Regression Estimate in Postcensal and Intercensal Population Estimation: A Case Study.* Rural Sociology, 1971. **36**: p. 187-194.

127. Keren, G. and J.R. Newman, *Additional considerations with regard to multiple regression and equal weighting.* Organizational Behaviour and Human Performance, 1978. **22**(2): p. 143-164.

128. Darlington, R.B., *Multiple Regression in Psychological Research and Practice.* Psychological Bulletin, 1968. **69**: p. 161-82.

129. Fourt, L.A. and J.W. Woodlock, *Early Prediction of Market Success for New Grocery Products.* Journal of Marketing, 1960(October): p. 31-38.

130. Cox, W.E., *Product life cycles as marketing models.* The Journal of Business, 1969. **40**(4): p. 375-384.

131. Harrell, G.D. and P.D. Bennett, *An Evaluation of the Expectancy Value Model of Attribute Measurement for Physician Prescribing Behavior.* Journal of Marketing Research, 1974. **11**: p. 269-78.

132. Juster, F., *Anticipations and Purchases: An Analysis of Consumer Behavior.* 1964, Princeton, NJ.: Princeton University Press.

133. Harrell, C.a.B., P., *An Evaluation of the Expectancy/Value Model of Attitude Measurement for Physician Prescribing Behavior.* Journal of Marketing Research, 1974. **11**: p. 269-78.

134. The Rand Corporation, *Submission to the Office of Management and Budget of Supporting Statement and Data Collection Instruments for Assessing the Effectiveness of the NIH Consensus Development Program.* 1983.

135. Blue Cross and Blue Shield Association, *Announcement of new phase of medical necessity program.* 1982: Chicago.

136. Zipf, G.K., *Human Behavior and the Principle of Least Effort.* 1949, Cambridge MA: Addison-Wesley.

137. Bond, R.S. and D.F. Lean, *Federal Trade Commission Staff Report on Sales, Promotion and Product Differentiation in Two Prescription Drug Markets.* 1977, Federal Trade Commission: Washington D. C.

138. Thomas, L.G., *Industrial Policy and International Competitiveness in the Pharmaceutical Industry,* in *Competitive Stategies in the Pharmaceutical Industry,* R.B. Helms, Editor. 1996, AEI Press: Washington.

139. Alpert, F.H. and M.A. Kamins, *An Empirical Investigation of Consumer Memory, Attitude, and Perceptions Toward Pioneer and Follower Brands.* Journal of Marketing, 1995. **59**: p. 34-45.

140. Hauser, J.R., *Competitive Price and Positioning Strategies.* Marketing Science, 1988. **7**(1): p. 76-91.

141. Schmalensee, R., *Product Differentiation Advantages of Pioneering Brands.* American Economic Review, 1982. **72**: p. 159-80.

142. Szymanski, D.M., L.C. Troy, and S.G. Bharadwaj, *Order of Entry and Business Performance: An Empirical Synthesis and Reexamination.* Journal of Marketing, 1995. **59**: p. 17-33.

143. Peckman, J.O., *The Wheel of Marketing.* 1978: Private Publication.

144. Daniels, J., *Waste just half your budget to win.* Pharmaceutical Marketing, 1997(July): p. 42-3.

145. Slywotzky, A.J. and B.P. Shapiro, *Leveraging to Beat the Odds: The New Marketing Mind-Set.* Harvard Business Review, 1993(September-October): p. 97-107.

146. O'Herlihy, C. and et al., *Long-Term Forecasts of Demand for Cars, Selected Consumer Durables and Energy.* National Institute Economic Review, 1967. **40**: p. 34-61.

147. Urban, G.L. and et al., *Market Share Rewards to Pioneering Brands: An Empirical Analysis and Strategic Implications.* Management Science, 1986. **32**(6): p. 645-59.

148. Rogers, E.M., *Diffusion of Innovation.* 1995, New York.: Free Press.

149. Bass, F.M., *A New Product Growth Model for Consumer Durables.* Management Science, 1969. **13**(5): p. 215-227.

150. Corstjens, M., *Marketing Strategy in the Pharmaceutical Industry.* 1991, London: International Thomson Business Press.

151. Walton, J., S. Adkins, and I. Smith, *Glaxo Wellcome.* 1998, Lehman Brothers: London.

152. Coleman, J. and et al., *The Diffusion of an Innovation Among Physicians.* Sociometry, 1957. **20**: p. 253-270.

153. Coleman, J.S. and et al., *Medical Innovation - A Diffusion Study.* 1966, New York: Bobbs-Merrill.

154. Peay, M.Y. and R. Edmund, *The Role of Commercial Sources in the Adoption of a New Drug.* Soc. Sci. Med., 1988. **26**(12): p. 1183-1189.

155. Williamson, P.M., *How general practitioners assess risks in using new drugs.* Journal of the Royal College of General Practitioners, 1975. **25**: p. 383.

156. Editorial, *Clinical trials and clinical practice.* The Lancet, 1993. **342**: p. 877-8.

157. Sultan, F., J.U. Farley, and D.R. Lehmann, *A Meta-Analysis of Diffusion Models.* Journal of Marketing Research, 1990. **37**: p. 70-77.

158. Boissel, J.-P., *Impact of Randomized Clinical Trials on Medical Practices.* Controlled Clinical Trails, 1989. **10**: p. 120S-134S.

159. Bass, F.M., *The Relationship between Diffusion Rates, Experience Curves, and Demand Elasticities for Consumer Durable Technological Innovations.* Journal of Business, 1980. **53**(Part 2 (July)): p. 51-68.

160. Horsky, D. and L.S. Simon, *Advertising and the Diffusion of New Products.* Marketing Science, 1983. **2**(1): p. 1-17.

161. Easingwood, C.J., V. Mahajan, and E. Muller, *A Nonuniform Influence Innovation Diffusion Model of New Product Acceptance.* Marketing Science, 1983. **2**(3): p. 273-295.

162. Norton, J.A., *Growth, Diffusion and Technological Substitution in Industrial Markets: An Examination of the Semi-Conductor Industry.* 1986, University Microfilms International: Ann Arbor: Michigan.

163. Salomon Brothers, *Posicor Report.* 1997, Salomon Brothers Analysts.

164. Lenk, P.J. and A.G. Rao, *New Models from Old: Forecasting Product Adoption by Hierarchical Bayes Proceedures.* Marketing Science, 1990. **9**(1): p. 42-53.

165. Sultan, F., J.U. Farley, and D.R. Lehmann, *A Meta-Analysis of Diffusion Studies.* Journal of Marketing Research, 1990. **XXVII**(February): p. 70-7.

166. Norton, J.A. and F.M. Bass, *Evolution of Technological Generations: The Law of Capture.* Sloan Management Review, 1992(Winter): p. 66-77.

167. Nakicenovic, N., *Software Package for the Logistic Substitution Model.* 1979, Laxenburg, Austria: International Institute for Applied Systems Analysis.

Index

A man ought to read just as inclination leads him,
For what he reads as a task will do him little good.
Samuel Johnson

An index of the key concepts and models in this book follows, to help you find what you need for your forecasting challenge

Action!

A thought that does not result in an action is nothing much and an action that does not proceed from a thought is nothing at all
Georges Barnardos

You can apply all the principles and all the models covered in this book to your own spreadsheet models with Inpharmation's EviCast, EviCast, EpiTree and phRISK technologies.

For more details, please contact...
Email: info@inpharmation.co.uk or
telephone : +44 1494 883458

Evidence Based Pricing Models

Get all the best validated pharma pricing models in a single package. PriceIT calculates the value that doctors and payers will place on any product in any country and any therapy area.

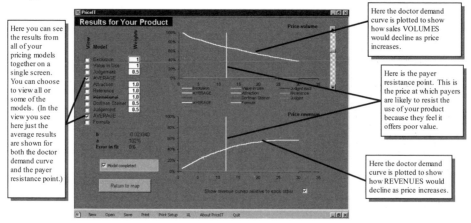

Here you can see the results from all of your pricing models together on a single screen. You can choose to view all or some of the models. (In the view you see here just the average results are shown for both the doctor demand curve and the payer resistance point.)

Here the doctor demand curve is plotted to show how sales VOLUMES would decline as price increases.

Here is the payer resistance point. This is the price at which payers are likely to resist the use of your product because they feel it offers poor value.

Here the doctor demand curve is plotted to show how REVENUES would decline as price increases.

International Pricing Strategy

PriceIT International is a powerful systems dynamics program that calculates all the interactions between countries (parallel trade, international price referencing) to allow you to establish the optimal global price strategy.

PriceIT International maps the full pattern of international price referencing for you.

INPHARMATION

Evidence based models

Long Meadow, Spurgrove Lane, Frieth,
Henley on Thames RG9 6NU England

Phone: **+44 1494 883458**

Fax: **+44 1494 882758**

E-mail: info@inpharmation.co.uk

Web: www.inpharmation.co.uk

Pharma Risk Analysis with phRISK

phRISK is the only risk analysis software specifically designed for pharma forecasters. Other risk analyzers are overly complex because they are designed to satisfy the needs of every industry that does risk modelling: nuclear power, electricity generation, oil exploration etc. etc. Most of this just confuses the pharma user. Now a crisp, powerful solution is available specifically for pharma forecasters...

phRISK is the first risk analyzer developed specifically for the pharma industry.

Rapid, cost-effective patient based forecasts

A simple and inexpensive way to estimate epi numbers, diagnosis rates and prescription rates that doesn't take months and cost a fortune. EpiTree provides 'good-enough' estimates for all your key patient based forecast assumptions in minutes!

EpiTree provides epi, diagnosis and prescription rate estimates for most diseases in minutes.

Implement Evidence Based Forecasting Now

The screenshot below shows you how one of the most powerful market share models can be combined with an uptake (diffusion) model to create powerful forecasts in minutes.

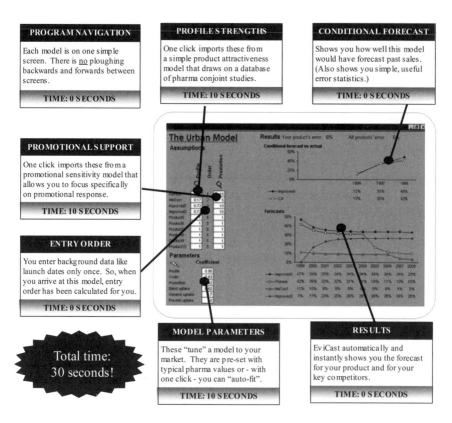

PROGRAM NAVIGATION

Each model is on one simple screen. There is no ploughing backwards and forwards between screens.

TIME: 0 SECONDS

PROFILE STRENGTHS

One click imports these from a simple product attractiveness model that draws on a database of pharma conjoint studies.

TIME: 10 SECONDS

CONDITIONAL FORECAST

Shows you how well this model would have forecast past sales. (Also shows you simple, useful error statistics.)

TIME: 0 SECONDS

PROMOTIONAL SUPPORT

One click imports these from a promotional sensitivity model that allows you to focus specifically on promotional response.

TIME: 10 SECONDS

ENTRY ORDER

You enter background data like launch dates only once. So, when you arrive at this model, entry order has been calculated for you.

TIME: 0 SECONDS

Total time: 30 seconds!

MODEL PARAMETERS

These "tune" a model to your market. They are pre-set with typical pharma values or - with one click - you can "auto-fit".

TIME: 10 SECONDS

RESULTS

EviCast automatically and instantly shows you the forecast for your product and for your key competitors.

TIME: 0 SECONDS

For more details on Inpharmation's forecasting technology – including free demos – please contact us. Contact details below.

INPHARMATION

Evidence based models
Long Meadow, Spurgrove Lane, Frieth,
Henley on Thames RG9 6NU England

Phone: +44 1494 883458

Fax: +44 1494 882758

E-mail: info@inpharmation.co.uk

Web: www.inpharmation.co.uk